Andy Rich

ASIAN HORROR

kamera
BOOKS

First published in 2010 by Kamera Books
PO Box 394, Harpenden, Herts, AL5 1XJ
www.kamerabooks.com

Copyright © Andy Richards 2010
Series Editor: Hannah Patterson

A CIP catalogue record for this book is available from the British Library.

ISBN 978-1-84243-320-1

2 4 6 8 10 9 7 5 3 1

Typeset by Elsa Mathern
Printed and bound in Great Britain by JF Print, Sparkford, Somerset

ACKNOWLEDGEMENTS

Grateful thanks to those editors and film critics who have nurtured my writing assignments over the years or merely offered their wisdom and encouragement: Leslie Felperin, Ed Lawrenson, Philip French, Mark Kermode, Nick Bradshaw, Tom Charity, Nick Duncalf, Dan Etherington, Anne Billson, Jamie Graham, Michael Bonner, Anne Hudson and Hannah Patterson.

Eternal gratitude to my ever-supportive parents and sisters, and extra special thanks to my wife Maddy – who eventually forgave me for taking her to see *Audition*, and to whom this book is lovingly dedicated.

CONTENTS

INTRODUCTION

Over the last decade, some of the sights and sounds of Asian horror have become so familiar to western audiences that they seem almost to have been reduced to a set of empty clichés and stock tricks: the haunted houses, creepy kids, ghosts in the machines, hands stretching from pools of brackish water, and, of course, all those lank-haired lady spooks, lurching jerkily towards the viewer's throat. By the time this stuff ends up being parodied in an instalment of the *Scary Movie* franchise, it has inevitably lost some of its original potency.

But it's easy to forget just what a potent shot in the arm for the horror genre the arrival of 'J-Horror' was at the dawn of the millennium. Hideo Nakata's *Ring* – a sensation on its release in Japan early in 1998 – premiered in the UK at the 2000 Edinburgh Film Festival (paired with its sequel *Ring 2*) alongside Takashi Miike's equally revelatory *Audition*. These two films went on to gain substantial international acclaim, returning Japanese horror cinema to the spotlight for the first time since the 1960s. A new generation of directors embarked on a full-scale revival of several styles of Japanese horror that had been popular in earlier eras – in particular the *kaidan eiga* (ghost-story film) that had flourished in the fifties and sixties – while adventurous distributors began riding this J-Horror wave, helping transform Japanese horror from a modest, home-grown business into a lucrative international industry. Other Asian countries followed Japan's lead, and new waves of horror were soon emerging from South Korea, Hong Kong and Thailand.

One of the benefits of the eastern horror boom has been to revive audience interest in some of the earlier landmarks of the genre; from cast-iron classics like Kenji Mizoguchi's *Tales of Ugetsu* (1953) and Kaneto Shindo's *Onibaba* (1964) to cult gems like Yasuzo Masumura's *Blind Beast* (1969), Asian horrors are now being appreciated afresh through lavish DVD reissues. This book is designed as an accessible overview of Asian horror cinema, highlighting some of the best examples of the genre from the 1950s to the present day. As well as exploring the production contexts and cultural backgrounds of seminal works like *Godzilla*, *Kwaidan*, *Ring*, *Ju-On: The Grudge*, *Audition*, *The Eye* and *A Tale of Two Sisters*, it also seeks to draw attention to less familiar, but no less rewarding, films like *Marebito*, *The Untold Story* and *Nang Nak*. Rather than attempting to be an encyclopaedic resource, this book aims rather to encourage readers to embark on their own explorations of some of the intriguing byways of Asian horror, while hopefully enhancing their appreciation of films they have already encountered.

This book also seeks to clarify some of the complexities of the mutually sustaining relationship between western and eastern horror cinema. When the new wave of Asian horror first broke with *Ring*, the films briefly found a home in mainstream cinemas, putting some of Hollywood's output at the time to shame. The likes of Nakata's superb *Dark Water* (2002) and Chan-wook Park's disturbing *Sympathy for Mr Vengeance* (2002) played in multiplexes alongside the exhausted antics of *Freddy vs Jason* (ironically directed by Asian émigré Ronny Yu), making it clear which way the wind was blowing. Hollywood was quick to take note, forking out for the remake rights to Asian horrors that had already proven their strong appeal for modern audiences seeking new types of scares. Starting with Gore Verbinski's lucrative remake of *Ring* in 2002, global audiences have been bombarded with a steady stream of glossy re-toolings of Asian originals – the majority of which have been serviceably scary but conspicuously inferior in execution to their sources. At the same time, many of the stylistic signatures of J-Horror (and its other Asian variants) were being cannibalised by Hollywood ghost films like *fear dot com* (2002), *The Amityville Horror* (2005) and *The Exorcism of Emily Rose* (2005).

Of course, some of these stylistic tics had appeared in American cinema (Adrian Lyne's *Jacob's Ladder* [1990] and David Lynch's *Twin Peaks: Fire Walk With Me* [1992] had already served up some terrifying, hallucinatory, jump-cut spookery), and American horror cinema wasn't entirely bereft of its own ideas at the point when *Ring* materialised. The jokey self-referentiality of the 1990s *Scream* franchise may have subjected the conventions of the slasher flick to merciless mockery, but the stylish gravitas of David Fincher's *Se7en* (1995) restored some of its sheen, while the phenomenal success of *The Blair Witch Project* (1999) proved that its own backwoods folklore could still provide grist for the US horror mill. As the millennium turned, American cinema also had a ghost boom of its own, with David Koepp's neglected Richard Matheson adaptation *Stir of Echoes* (1999), M Night Shyamalan's *The Sixth Sense* (1999) and Alejandro Amenabar's *The Others* (2001) delivering subtle supernatural chills closer to the spirit of Val Lewton than George Romero. It made sense, then, that the audiences for these films would also prove receptive to Asian horror cinema – with its venerable traditions of ghost stories – and that Asian films would provide rich pickings for Hollywood remakes. With most filmmakers nowadays being highly international in their outlook and interests, the ebb and flow of influence and counter-influence can be tough to trace. In an intriguing recent instance of cross-cultural synergy, Jason Cuadrado's 2007 ghost anthology film *Tales from the Dead* was devised as a Japanese-language, J-Horror film which – bizarrely – was shot entirely in Los Angeles using local Japanese talent!

Despite all the cross-pollination between eastern and western horror in recent years, it's clear that Asian horror films have characteristics that differentiate them from their western counterparts. These vary greatly between subgenres and regions, but in general involve a more fatalistic tone, a more pessimistic approach to an individual's control over their destiny, a more profound sense of the presence of supernatural forces in the 'real' world, and a willingness – allied with a lack of squeamishness – to push horrific imagery to graphic extremes. As this book will hopefully demonstrate, these qualities have their origins in complex Asian cultural traditions, while the films frequently explore themes that are specifically rooted in the turbulent histories of the countries that created them.

Inevitably, Japan dominates any discussion of Asian horror cinema, and the bulk of the cultural background explored in this book relates to that country. However, South Korea, Thailand and Hong Kong have all been important sources of horror cinema in recent years, and separate chapters deal with their specific cultures. This book focuses on the East Asian countries that have experienced the most significant horror booms in recent years, to the exclusion of India, Malaysia, Singapore, the Philippines and other Asian territories whose horror films – while being of considerable interest – have not matched the international impact of East Asian horror.

People's understanding of what constitutes a 'horror film' can differ widely. This book surveys a broad range of movies whose primary aims are to terrify or disturb audiences – many featuring elements of the supernatural, but plenty dealing with more purely psychological (or psychotic) terrors. Slasher, serial-killer and rape-revenge films are part of this landscape, as are some of the more experimental excursions into cyberpunk, splatterpunk and body horror territory. Asian horror frequently revels in its own pick-and-mix approach to genre, and, indeed, its unwillingness to be confined within conventional genre boundaries is a crucial part of its audience appeal (as with Miike's *Audition* or Ryuhei Kitamura's *Versus*). Many Hong Kong horror films blend their spooks and gore with slapstick comedy, sentimental romance and acrobatic combat, while some of the most exciting Korean offerings of recent years – notably Chan-wook Park's celebrated 'Vengeance Trilogy' – deliberately sidestep easy labels.

Sadly, in 2008, the distributor Tartan Films – which had done so much in the last decade to boost the popularity of Asian horror cinema in the West – folded its operations in the UK and the US, and its library of films was bought by the US-based Palisades Media Group. It remains to be seen what this will mean for the future acquisition and distribution of Asian horror titles.

A brief note on names and titles: for the sake of clarity, this book refers to films where possible by their English-language-release titles – adding an Asian transliterated title in the more detailed review sections – e.g. Hideo Nakata's *Ring* (*Ringu*, 1998). Names of directors, producers, writers, stars and story characters follow the western ordering convention – with forenames preceding family names.

THIN PARTITIONS:
ASIA & THE SUPERNATURAL

"I've heard this sentence: the partition that separates life from death does not appear so thick to us as it does to a westerner."
Chris Marker's *Sans Soleil* (1983)

Cultural generalisations can be perilous undertakings, but there are significant ways in which contemporary eastern cultures demonstrate a more widespread and engrained acceptance of supernatural forces than their western counterparts. The roots of this lie in Asian religious traditions (Buddhism and Shinto, for example), whose animistic, pantheistic and karmic beliefs contrast sharply with the more binary moralities of the western Judeo-Christian tradition. According to Shinto, for instance, millions of Japanese objects – from trees, rocks and rivers to commonplace domestic items – are inhabited by spirit deities, which in varying circumstances can prove friendly or aggressive. Spirits are not necessarily seen as antagonists or entities that should be eliminated, but as beings that co-exist with the world of the living.

There are various concrete examples of modern-day Asian cultural practices that reflect this sense of the porous boundaries and free-flowing interplay between the material world and the afterlife. Many Japanese homes contain a *butsudan* (Buddhist household altar), where the spirits of dead relatives are supposed to reside, and to whom regular offerings are made. Many South Koreans regularly consult with Shamanistic *mudangs*, who dispense advice on matters of the heart and perform rituals or exorcisms. As a result of these active religious traditions, eastern cultures are saturated with ghost stories to a much greater degree than those of the West – stories which dominate their visual, literary and theatrical heritage, as well as their cinematic traditions.

SUPERNATURAL STORYTELLING

Japanese literature contains a long tradition of supernatural storytelling that draws on the ghosts and demons of Shinto and Buddhism. A major touchstone was the eleventh-century *The Tale of Genji*, whose jealous Lady Rokujo is a prototype for the unquiet spirit – or *yurei* – that would become such a crucial component of Japanese mythology (and virtually a cliché of J-Horror). *Yurei* come into being when people die violently through suicide or murder, or in the grip of passionate emotions, or if fitting burial rites have not been adequately performed. Almost invariably female, *yurei* tend to float while dressed in white Shinto burial *kimonos*, hands dangling limply, with a single baleful eye staring through sheets of long, scraggly black hair (Japanese women traditionally pinned their hair up, but it was let down for burial). Vengeance-driven *yurei* were sub-categorised as *onryou*, and their murderous retribution would often not merely be restricted to those who had wronged them (a tradition that would memorably extend to the ghostly Kayako in *Ju-On: The Grudge* [2002]).

Another entity that has recurred throughout the history of Japanese horror is the *bakeneko* ('cat demon') – a creature capable of possessing people, created when a cat licks the blood of its murdered owner. Wells are another classic trope, and are frequently used as places for concealing corpses. This stratagem is used by the samurai Aoyama in one classic folktale – he kills his maid, Okiku, after she rejects his overtures, only to be tormented by her disconsolate wails from the depths of her watery grave. Water is often seen as a gateway to the underworld – as demonstrated by the floating of lanterns during the annual *O-Bon* Japanese Buddhist festival honouring ancestral spirits.

Japan's Edo period (1603–1867) was the golden age of the *kaidan* (ghost story), when authors like Ogita Ansei, Asai Ryoi and Ueda Akinari (sometimes referred to as the Japanese Maupassant) perfected the form. These were usually based on didactic Buddhist stories or folk legends (sometimes taken from plays), and *onryou* and haunted houses were commonly featured. One Edo parlour game called *Hyakumonogatari Kaidankai* involved players sitting in a room with a hundred lit candles and extinguishing them one at a time after recounting a series of *kaidan* (the final candle was believed to summon a spirit). The phenomenal popularity of this game – combined with new printing technology – led to ghost stories being collected and published from all parts of Japan (and the transplantation of Chinese folktales to Japan). Later writers like Lafcadio Hearn (1850–1904) and Junichiro Tanizaki (1886–1965) created anthologised collections of the nation's folktales, providing a wellspring for films like Masaki Kobayashi's *Kwaidan* (1964). The writings of Hirai Taro (1894–1965) – who adopted the pen name Edogawa Rampo, an oriental rendering of the name of his literary idol Edgar Allan Poe (try saying it out loud) – would be a major influence on the later *ero-gro* ('erotic-grotesque') subgenre of films.

Many *kaidan* story motifs were absorbed into – and simultaneously drew from – Japan's performing arts traditions. The repertoire of *Noh* theatre – a style originating in the fourteenth century – boasts over 200 plays, many with supernatural elements. These highly stylised blends of music, drama and dance, designed for the ruling classes, were enacted in a minimalist, semi-abstract fashion by a pair of (usually masked) performers. Prominent categories include *shura-mono* (ghost plays) and *shunen-mono* (revenge plays), which would often combine in stories of otherworldly retribution, frequently involving vengeful *yurei*. Transformations were often part of the narratives (in *Yamanba*, for example, a humble old lady mutates into an *onibaba*, or demon woman); undead warriors were another trope – plays like *Funa-Benkei* anticipate the otherworldly clashes of Kitamura's *Versus* (2000) by centuries. Often, characters known as *waki* – usually wandering priests – would appear and offer warnings to the principal characters about ghosts or curses.

A later form of Japanese theatre, *Kabuki*, was less elitist than *Noh*, and had an even more direct impact on later horror cinema. First developed in the seventeenth century, *Kabuki* drew on *Noh* plays for some of its stories and style, but was an altogether more elaborate type of theatrical experience. It developed complicated systems of trapdoors, passageways, hidden wires, pulleys, water pits and revolving stages to create slick theatrical illusions that were the precursors of modern cinematic SFX (its legacy reflected perhaps in the DIY effects of Ishiro Honda's seminal 1954 *Godzilla*). *Kaidan* were a popular *Kabuki* genre – *The Ghost Story of Yotsuya*, first performed in 1821, being probably the most famous. Visual shorthands for representing *yurei* were developed – including a white burial kimono, wild black hair and white-and-indigo face makeup. Transformations were again a recurring theme: in *Tsuchigumo*, a young boy is revealed to be a monstrous spider demon. There were also strong streaks of brutality and cruelty in *Kabuki* – torture, mutilation and suicide were regular elements – that find many echoes in later horror cinema.

The visual arts have also been a rich source of the horrific imagery that fed into horror cinema. Buddhist temple paintings and twelfth-century *jigoku-zoshi* (Hell scroll paintings) contained graphic depictions of the torments of the underworld, administered by grotesque demons. The first known image of a *yurei* was in Okyo Maruyama's painting *The Ghost of Oyuki*, and Tokyo's Zenshoan Temple now has a collection of 50 nineteenth-century silk scroll paintings depicting *yurei*. Another key source of inspiration was the tradition of *Ukiyo-e* (the 'floating world' genre of woodblock prints), which contained vividly colourful and physically graphic depictions of mythological ghosts, demons and *yurei* alongside domestic scenes. Katsushika Hokusai was one of the most celebrated exponents, and his series of nineteenth-century prints, *One Hundred Tales*, includes such choice sights as an *onibaba* eating the decapitated head of a baby, while the artist Yoshitoshi depicted scenes of mutilation and the torture of captive women plucked directly from his era's grisly civil war. Elsewhere, *Ukiyo-e* images of water dragons can be found that anticipate the appearance of Godzilla. The work of artists like Hokusai, Hiroshige and Kuniyoshi – which they sometimes bound together in notebooks – is a precursor of the work of modern-day *manga* artists, a key influence on contemporary horror films.

JAPANESE HORROR FILMS: MODERNISM & MONSTERS

Examples of Japanese horror cinema can be found from as early as 1898, when shorts like *Jizo the Ghost* and *Resurrection of a Corpse* were produced. But it wasn't until after the Second World War that the genre would really take flight. Horror films have always tended to reflect the dominant social anxieties of the time and place in which they are produced, and the post-war era was a particularly turbulent one for Japan: the country had suffered a humiliating military defeat, entailing catastrophic casualties (2.7 million dead and a huge number missing or wounded). Hundreds of thousands had perished in the nuclear obliterations of Hiroshima and Nagasaki and their radioactive aftermaths. Humiliatingly, after its defeat Japan was placed under occupation by US troops for the next seven years and prevented from re-arming.

The sheer scale of Japan's wartime destruction found its most obvious mirror in the *kaiju eiga* ('monster movie') cycle of the 1950s, with *Godzilla* (1954) leading the charge. This film, along with its numerous sequels and imitators, would ritualistically re-enact the destruction of Tokyo (which had been saturation-bombed by the Allies), while the parade of mutant beasts was a blatant reminder of the horrors of radiation damage and environmental pollution. Fears of apocalyptic destruction have been a constant theme of Japanese horror through to the present day, while scarred female faces (a common sight on nuclear-bomb victims) find their way into a number of horror films – from *Ghost Story of Yotsuya* (1959) and *Onibaba* (1964) to *Face of Another* (1966) and *Imprint* (2006).

As commentators like Colette Balmain have noted, during the occupation period the country's traditional value system collided head-on with the forces of western modernisation. The Shinto codes that the nation had been built on – based on Confucian ethics setting out complex sets of reciprocal responsibilities between the emperor and his subjects, and between family members and friends – were replaced by western democratic values and a new emphasis on capitalist individualism. Many of the Japanese horror films produced in the 1950s dramatised this collision in coded form: the selfish pursuit of personal gain at the expense of collective values lies at the root of the ghostly tragedies of *Tales of Ugetsu* and *Ghost Story of Yotsuya*, for example.

BOOM TIME FOR EDO GOTHIC

In the fifties and sixties, while Britain was thrilling to its Hammer horrors and America to its AIP Poe cycle, Japan was enjoying its own Gothic boom. These *kaidan eiga* ('ghost story films', a term with an archaic flavour redolent of the Edo era) were usually based on *Kabuki* plays or Buddhist folk tales set during the Edo (or occasionally the subsequent Meiji) period. The big-name player in this movement was the director Nobuo Nakagawa, who racked up a string of successes for Shintoho Studios, including *The Ghosts of Kasane Swamp* (1957) and *Ghost Story of Yotsuya* (1959). Other notable examples of the genre included Masaki Mori's *Ghost of Kagama-Ga-Fuchi* (1959) and Satsuo Yamamoto's *The Bride From Hell* (1968), the latter adapted from the oft-filmed folktale *The Peony Lantern*, an archetypal story of doomed love featured in an 1892 *Kabuki* play. Staple story elements of the *kaidan eiga* included vaultingly ambitious *ronin* (masterless samurai) betraying their *bushido* codes, adultery, conspiracy and revenge – with wronged women frequently returning from the graves as *onryou* to torment the feckless men who abused their trust. Also cropping up regularly in these films was the folkloric feline *bakeneko*, gracing Yoshiro Ishikawa's *The Ghost Cat of Otama Pond* (1960) and Kaneto Shindo's *Kuroneko* (1968).

During this period, some of the more prestigious Japanese horror films met with considerable international success: Mizoguchi's *Tales of Ugetsu* (1953), Masaki Kobayashi's *Kwaidan* (1964) and Kaneto Shindo's *Onibaba* (1964) were all eye-openers for western audiences in the same way that Nakata's *Ring* would be several decades later.

WESTERN BORROWINGS

As well as this rich seam of home-grown material, Japanese horror filmmakers also mined the western horror classics for ideas, producing several blatantly orientalised reworkings. Hajime Sato came up with *The Ghost of the Hunchback* (1965), while Michio Yamamoto directed a trilogy of Hammer homages – *Legacy of Dracula* (1970), *Lake of Dracula* (1971) and *Evil of Dracula* (1974). These kind of cross-cultural borrowings have often been beneficial to the development of cinematic genres: American and European Westerns were certainly enriched by the influence of Japanese classics like Kurosawa's *The Bodyguard* (1961) and *The Seven Samurai* (1954) (themselves influenced by John Ford, and respectively remade as Leone's *A Fistful of Dollars* [1964] and Sturges' *The Magnificent Seven* [1960]). Japanese horror cinema, meanwhile, has always been open to influences from the West – from Edo Gothic's debt to the lurid period horrors of Hammer and Corman to the Dario Argento-inspired mayhem of *Evil Dead Trap* (1988), the Tobe Hooper nods in Shugo Fujii's *Living Hell: A Japanese Chainsaw Massacre* (2000) and the pervasive influence of Kubrick's *The Shining* on much modern J-Horror (Takashi Shimizu's 2005 *Reincarnation* being only the most overt in its borrowings).

CLASSIC JAPANESE HORRORS
1953–1968

Tales of Ugetsu/Ugetsu Monogatari (1953)

Directed by: Kenji Mizoguchi
Cast: Masayuki Mori (Genjuro), Machiko Kyo (Lady Wakasa), Mitsuko Mito (Ohama), Kinuyo Tanaka (Miyagi), Sakae Ozawa (Tobei)

Story

The action is set in the sixteenth century, in a province ravaged by civil war. Genjuro, a potter, leaves his wife and son to try and sell his wares. The pots are bought by Lady Wakasa, who invites Genjuro to her home, Kutsuki Manor. There she seduces and then marries him, telling him that he must devote his entire life to her. An itinerant monk warns Genjuro that his life and soul are in danger because his new wife is actually a ghost – the last trace of a decimated noble clan. After having a Buddhist exorcism performed, Genjuro flees the Manor and returns to his wife, Ohama, who welcomes him home. The next morning, he is informed that his wife has been killed earlier by marauding soldiers. He realises that he was welcomed home by her ghost, who wanted to reunite him with his son. In a separate plotline, Genjuro's peasant neighbour, Tobei, bluffs his way to becoming a renowned samurai, although he nearly loses his wife Miyagi in the process.

Background

Snapping up the Silver Lion at the 1953 Venice Film Festival, Mizoguchi's masterpiece (one of many) was part of the first wave of Japanese art-house cinema – preceded by Akira Kurosawa's *Rashomon* (1950) – that wowed international audiences in the early fifties. *Tales of Ugetsu* is based on the short stories 'The House in the Thicket', in which a man is welcomed home by the ghost of his dead wife, and 'A Serpent's Lust', which features a vengeful female spirit. These both appeared in Ueda Akinari's 1776 *kaidan* collection *Tales of Moonlight and Rain* (sourced from Chinese originals), and *Tales of Ugetsu* combines them with the separate Tobei subplot, drawn from a Maupassant story.

Like other Japanese directors in the post-war period, Mizoguchi (1898–1956) was able to take advantage of the loosening of censorship restrictions – on erotic material, at any rate – that had taken place during the US occupation (which had only ended the year before this film's release). This allowed him to create some wonderfully sensual sequences in which Genjuro is seduced by the ghostly Lady Wakasa. Her appearance in these scenes is directly modelled on the stylised masks of *Noh* theatre, as is the courtly dance that she performs for the hapless potter. Akira Kurosawa – with whom Mizoguchi felt a keen professional rivalry – would be influenced by *Tales of Ugetsu* in his use of *Noh* conventions to depict the supernatural elements in his *Macbeth* adaptation *Throne of Blood* (1957).

Verdict

As far removed from a Takashi Miike gore-fest as you can get, this film occupies the gentler and more refined end of the Asian horror spectrum. Its status as a cast-iron supernatural classic remains firm, though, thanks to Mizoguchi's breathtaking staging of the enchantment scenes at Kutsuki Manor. The director uses his famously fluid camera style to convey the eerie otherworldliness of the setting, while clever lighting and makeup send subtle chills through the viewer as we watch Genjuro fall ever more deeply under the ghost's spell. It's the masterful combination of these sequences of poetic fantasy with the painful realism of the film's brutal scenes of wartime rape and violence that gives the film its enduring power.

Ultimately, Mizoguchi was more concerned with reflecting the social dislocations and misguided militarism that his country had undergone in the preceding years than in creating a full-blooded *kaidan eiga* of the kind that Nobuo Nakagawa would perfect in the coming years. His film reflects a fear of the modernity encroaching on post-war Japanese society, in which individualism and materialism were replacing the Shinto social obligations (particularly towards women) of earlier eras. Nevertheless, some key tropes of Japanese horror films – the haunted house, doomed love, the beautiful female ghost – find early cinematic expression here, and the film serves as a template for many later 'erotic' ghost-story films featuring supernatural seductions, from Chusei Sone's *Hellish Love* (1972) to Siu-Tung Ching's Hong Kong classic *A Chinese Ghost Story* (1987).

Godzilla/Gojira (1954)

Directed by: Ishiro Honda
Cast: Takeshi Shimura (Professor Yamane), Akira Takarada (Ogata), Momoko Kochi (Emiko Yamane), Akihiro Harata (Dr Serizawa)

Story

Several ships are sunk off the coast of Japan's Odo Island in mysterious circumstances. A research party headed by palaeontologist Professor Yamane visits the island to investigate, where they encounter Godzilla – a 50-metre-tall radioactive lizard from the Jurassic era that has been awakened from the ocean depths by American H-bomb tests. Yamane is eager to study Godzilla and learn from it, but the monster attacks Tokyo. The military are powerless against the creature, and it causes widespread death and destruction with its atomic breath and gargantuan size. Reluctantly, the enigmatic Dr Serizawa is convinced to use an 'Oxygen Destroyer' that he has developed to kill Godzilla, deliberately sacrificing himself in the process to prevent his scientific secrets from falling into irresponsible hands.

Background

Toho Studios' seminal *kaiju eiga* movie spawned a long-running franchise of lurid psychedelic head-to-heads featuring its reptilian antagonist pitted against a range of outlandish foes including Mothra, Ghidorah and Mechagodzilla, but the monochrome Japanese original is a different beast altogether. On its domestic release, the nuclear devastation of Hiroshima and Nagasaki – as well as the US bombing raids made over Tokyo in March 1945 – were fresh wounds on the national psyche, while the nuclear arms race (which the film angrily critiques) was shifting into high gear. In fact, the film was made in the same year that the US tested an H-bomb at Bikini Atoll in the Pacific, showering a nearby Japanese tuna trawler – the *Lucky Dragon* – with radioactive debris (an event overtly referenced in *Godzilla*'s opening sequences).

Director Ishiro Honda (1911–93), a friend and collaborator of Akira Kurosawa, served in World War Two and did time as a POW in mainland China in 1945, passing through the ruins of Hiroshima after the war ended. After the success of *Godzilla* he became a sci-fi specialist, helming several other *kaiju eiga*, including *Rodan* (1956) and *Dogora the Space Monster* (1965), using the genre to explore anti-war themes. The film's special-effects work was masterminded by Eiji Tsuburaya, who became Japan's foremost SFX guru. Budgetary and time restrictions, as well as a lack of expertise, meant that he was unable to depict Godzilla using the stop-motion effects he had so admired in the original *King Kong* (1933), but he achieved a great deal using miniature work, optical effects and a man in a rubber suit (or 'Suitmation' as it became affectionately known). Limited resources also stirred the creative juices of composer Akira Ifukube, who generated the monster's famous roar by scraping a bass fiddle string with a glove.

Godzilla was influenced by popular American monster movies of the era (particularly *The Beast from 20,000 Fathoms*, 1953), so it was perhaps inevitable that the US would want to serve up Honda's film as their own style of monster mash. The Japanese original was acquired by an American distributor who shortened, dubbed and heavily re-edited the film, inserting new sequences with a news correspondent (played by Raymond Burr) and cutting out most of the references to Hiroshima, Nagasaki and the monster's nuclear awakening. This inferior version was released as *Godzilla: King of the Monsters* in 1956 ('Dynamic Violence! Savage Action! Spectacular Thrills!'), beginning the monster's iconic success in western culture as well as eastern.

Verdict

The most striking aspect of this original – certainly when set against the cartoonish later instalments in the series – is its emphasis on the human damage caused by the rampaging monster. Given that Godzilla itself is a coded metaphor for the atomic threat, this film is one of the only Japanese movies of the period to depict the effects of nuclear holocaust on a civilian population. Made very soon after the Allied occupation of Japan ended, it expresses some of the repressed pain and horror that people felt at their country's devastation. As later Asian horror films would confirm (notably *The Host*, 2006), *Godzilla* demonstrates that a giant monster movie is one of the most effective ways of dramatising social, political and ecological crises.

Ghost Story of Yotsuya/Tokaido Yotsuya Kaidan (1959)

Directed by: Nobuo Nakagawa
Cast: Shigeru Amachi (Iemon), Katsuko Wakasugi (Iwa), Junko Ikeuchi (Ume), Noriko Kitazawa (Samon)

Story

Destitute *ronin* Iemon marries Iwa after secretly murdering her disapproving father. They have a child together, but Iemon is unable to stomach their life of poverty and starts to think he'd be better off married to wealthy Ume. Egged on by his nefarious servant Naosuke, he hatches a plan to kill Iwa after framing her for adultery. Hideously mutilated by the poison he administers, Iwa is driven to kill herself and their baby. Unfortunately for Iemon, she then returns as an *onryou*, intent on destroying all shreds of his sanity.

Background

There have been some 30 screen adaptations of Tsuruya Namboku's smash-hit 1821 *Kabuki* play, based on a folktale, which – *Ring* notwithstanding – remains perhaps the most famous Japanese ghost story of all time. The first silent version appeared back in 1912, while *Battle Royale* director Kinji Fukasaku made a version in 1994. Nakagawa's 1959 classic isn't the most faithful version of the material (an honour that probably falls to 1966's *Illusion of Blood*), but it's justly celebrated as the most impressive.

Nakagawa (1905–84) was the first true master of Japanese horror, and during the fifties and sixties he firmly established the *kaidan eiga* as a mainstay of Japanese cinema. Sometimes dubbed 'the Nippon Hitchcock', he notched up nearly 100 films in an eclectic career stretching back to the silent era. Other horror highlights from his prolific filmography include *The Ghosts of Kasane Swamp* (1957), based on an eighteenth-century vampire tale, *The Mansion of the Ghost Cat* (1958), *The Lady Vampire* (1959), *Hell* (1960) and *Snake Woman's Curse* (1968). Many of his horror pics were made at the slightly disreputable Shintoho Studios (sometimes compared to Hollywood's cut-price Republic Pictures), which had splintered off from the prestigious Toho Company and – helmed by ambitious executive and former carnival showman Mitsugu Okura – became specialists in exploitation fare.

Verdict

The brilliance of Nakagawa's film lies in the combination of the classical elegance of its folkloric storytelling with its grisly visual effects. The sight of Iwa's rotting face, rendered in glorious colour, is unforgettable, while a scene in which Iemon lops off an adversary's limb (which then lies twitching on the ground) is strikingly violent for the pre-sixties. With her white burial *kimono*, long dishevelled hair and freakish eyes, Iwa is an all-time classic *yurei*, and a clear model for *Ring*'s fiendish Sadako.

Hell/Jigoku (1960)

Directed by: Nobuo Nakagawa
Cast: Shigeru Amachi (Shiro), Yoichi Numata (Tamura), Utako Mitsuya (Yukiko/Sachiko)

Story

College student Shiro is involved in a hit-and-run with a drunken *yakuza* while out driving with his volatile friend, Tamura. Soon after, Shiro's fiancée, Yukiko, is killed in a separate car accident. Shiro heads to provincial Tenjoen, where his father runs the Senior Citizens' Facility, to visit his dying mother. The Facility is a den of debauchery, frequented by his father's mistress, a criminally negligent doctor, a lecherous cop and a drunken painter. Shiro falls for the painter's daughter, Sachiko, who looks identical to Yukiko. With the arrival of Tamura and the *yakuza*'s vengeful moll, however, events descend into total chaos: Shiro discovers that Sachiko is his relative, and a bizarre mass poisoning kills most of the cast. Several of the characters then find themselves in Hell, where Shiro tries desperately to redeem the soul of his unborn child (who died with Yukiko) while grotesque tortures are inflicted by demons on the various sinners.

Background

Hell was the last of the string of horror films that Nakagawa made at Shintoho, and in fact the company went bust soon after this production. Originally, the film was conceived as 'Heaven and Hell', but somewhere along the line the 'Heaven' element got dropped, leaving Nakagawa free to concentrate on a vision of Hell derived from Buddhist temple paintings and twelfth-century *jigoku-zoshi* ('Hell scroll paintings'), as well as descriptions of the torments of the underworld in *Ojoyoshu*, written by the Buddhist monk Genshin in the tenth century. Nakagawa retained composer Chumei Watanabe and production designer Harayusa Kurosawa from the previous year's *Ghost Story of Yotsuya*, as well as lead actor Shigeru Amachi. There were Japanese remakes of *Hell* in 1979 by Tatsumi Kumashiro and in 1999 by Teruo Ishii, and in Thailand it was re-jigged as *Narok* (2005).

Verdict

Playing as a kind of *Faust*-meets-*Hellraiser*, Hell is a truly bizarre viewing experience. Blending ancient Buddhist lore with the hip 'Scope stylings of the Japanese New Wave, it takes the viewer to some very strange places. Admittedly, the storytelling isn't as streamlined as it could be (the Mephistophelian Tamura's role is never satisfyingly defined), but the film more than compensates for its occasional incoherence with the sheer lurid inventiveness of its vision of the lower depths. The parade of miscreant souls, having crossed the Sanzu River and been damned by the Judge of Hell, are variously mutilated, flayed and decapitated, while the flaming Buddhist Wheel of Life spins inexorably on.

This gonzo gore-fest, however, is only the corporeal culmination of the film's explorations of various other types of 'hell': that of a corrupt society (the dumping ground for the elderly run by Shiro's father is decadent and vice-ridden); that of individual guilt (Shiro fails to turn himself in after the hit-and-run, despite his moral misgivings);

and that of psychological pain (Shiro loses his fiancée and child). Like many of the best Asian horror films, this one inhabits the fertile ground between art and exploitation, happy to combine Buddhist musings on transience and karmic retribution with the visceral shocks of its torments of the damned.

Onibaba (1964)

Directed by: Kaneto Shindo
Cast: Nobuko Otowa (Older Woman), Jitsuko Yoshimura (Younger Woman), Kei Sato (Hachi)

Story

During a bloody sixteenth-century civil war, an elderly woman and her daughter-in-law survive by murdering passing *samurai* and trading their armour for rice. They dispose of their victims' bodies down a deep pit in the middle of the tall-grass fields that surround their hut. When the younger woman starts an affair with Hachi, a neighbouring farmer, the older woman not only becomes fearful that she will be abandoned by her partner-in-crime and starve, but is also consumed by sexual jealousy. She tries to dissuade the girl from her nightly trysts by dressing up in a stolen demon mask and scaring her senseless, only to belatedly discover that the mask inflicts a horrific curse on its wearers.

Background

Kaneto Shindo, like Nakagawa, was a prolific force in Japanese film. Born in 1912, he was apprenticed to Mizoguchi in the thirties, fought in World War Two, and co-founded an independent production company in 1950. He went on to direct over 40 features based on his own screenplays, and, at the time of writing, is still going strong in his mid-nineties.

Onibaba was based on a Buddhist fable called *A Mask with Flesh Scared a Wife*, which was actually about a mother trying to dissuade her daughter from being *virtuous*. By shifting the focus firmly onto *vice* (particularly lust) and making his actresses (including his wife and muse Nobuko Otowa as the mother-in-law) spend a good part of the film bare-breasted, Shindo aroused the prurient interest of an international audience, and created the first Japanese horror film to gain a significant worldwide release.

Shindo wanted to set the film in fields of swaying *susuki* (pampas grass) to intensify the sense of erotic frisson, and sourced a suitable location in the Inba Swamp region outside Tokyo. The cast and crew camped out in pre-fab huts for the duration of the shoot, which was plagued by typhoons, flooding and infestations of crustaceans and bugs.

Verdict

Shindo's location gambit paid off in spades, helping create an atmosphere thick with carnal desire and the threat of violence. *Onibaba* presents a vision of a society regressing to its most savage, base state. Like Ingmar Bergman's *The Seventh Seal* (1957) and *The Virgin Spring* (1960), or his mentor Mizoguchi's *Sansho the Bailiff* (1954), Shindo uses a medieval setting to explore human behaviour at its most essential, when the veneer of civilisation has been ruthlessly stripped away. The older woman in the story may receive a terrible supernatural punishment for her murderous venality, but it's always clear that war has severely limited her options for survival. The human struggles in the film feel gritty and realistic, but the film is also pregnant with rich symbolism. As well as the sensually swaying *susuki*, there's the mysterious *Noh* mask (evoking Buddhist damnation) and the deep, dark hole at the heart of the story – conjuring thoughts of death, hell and the abyss of carnal desire.

With its high-contrast, black-and-white 'Scope images, *Onibaba* delivers some startling visual coups: many of the painterly tableaux . are composed like Japanese inkbrush paintings, while the lightning-fast horizontal tracking shots (as characters run through the wind-blown grass) are simply stunning to behold. The exciting percussive score on *taiko* (Japanese drums) by Hikaru Hyashi is the final crucial ingredient in Shindo's ambitious and wholly successful attempt to – in his own words – 'show sexual desire within the soul'.

Kwaidan/Kaidan (1964)

Directed by: Masaki Kobayashi
Cast: Rentaro Mikuni (Samurai), Tatsuya Nakadai (Woman in the Snow), Katsuo Nakamura (Hoichi)

Story

An anthology of four stories adapted from Lafcadio Hearn's folkloric *kaidan* collections. In 'The Black Hair', an impoverished *samurai* in old Kyoto divorces his wife and marries the daughter of a noble family to acquire position. Consumed by guilt, he returns to his first wife and they spend the night together. The next morning, he awakes to discover he has slept beside a rotted skeleton, whose hair then takes on a vengeful life of its own. His wife, it transpires, has died following the divorce, and his home has been abandoned for years. In 'The Woman of the Snow', a pair of woodcutters are overtaken by a snowstorm. They encounter a ghostly woman, who kills the elderly woodcutter with her icy breath. She takes pity on his apprentice, however, and spares him on condition that he never reveal what happened that day. Ten years later, the apprentice finds himself spilling the beans to his wife, who transforms into the ghost woman. In 'Hoichi the Earless', a blind Buddhist monk is recruited to perform a song-cycle for a mysterious lord and his court. Each night, he sings of an epic sea battle from 700 years ago in which two clans perished. Hoichi's fellow monks are concerned when his health begins to deteriorate, and one evening they follow him to an old cemetery and discover that he has been playing for the ghostly casualties of the sea battle. His master tries to save Hoichi by painting him with calligraphic charms to ward off the ghosts, but unfortunately forgets to daub his ears. 'In a Cup of Tea' tells of a man who drinks an image of a *samurai* reflected in his cup.

Background

Masaki Kobayashi (1916–96) was an avowed pacifist and made several powerful films about World War Two and its aftermath (he served, as well as spending time as a POW). With his first colour film, *Kwaidan*, he also made a significant contribution to the horror genre, drawing on his background in painting and the fine arts to mount a meticulously crafted compendium of home-grown ghost stories. The film was his first independent production after years of contract work for Shochiku studios.

Verdict

Horror anthologies can be notoriously ropey affairs – witness George Romero's *Creepshow* (1982) or Freddie Francis's *Dr Terror's House of Horrors* (1965) – but Kobayashi's film remains a triumph of spooky storytelling. These stories may not freeze the blood in the way that *Onibaba* or *Hell* do, but each is eerily atmospheric and a true feast for the senses. Indulging his interest in Japanese art, the backdrops to Kobayashi's stylised, deliberately artificial sets (filmed in a converted aircraft hanger) are all painted in vivid colours, filling the Toho 'Scope frame with a riot of expressionistic excess. As with other Japanese horrors of the era, the score is crucial to the overall effect, and Toru Takemitsu's experimental music doesn't disappoint. The film's opening episode has clear story parallels with Mizoguchi's *Tales of Ugetsu*, while the spectral black hair that rises at its climax to throttle the errant husband clearly anticipates the long-haired horrors of the *Ring* and *Ju-On* cycles. The 'Hoichi' episode, meanwhile, is strongly influenced by *Noh* theatrical practice, with its blind protagonist retelling the story of a military defeat to the accompaniment of his *biwa* instrument.

Kuroneko/Yabu no Naka no Kuroneko (1968)

Directed by: Kaneto Shindo
Cast: Kichiemon Nakamura (Gintoki), Nobuko Otowa (Yone), Kiwako Taichi (Shige), Hideo Kanze (Mikado)

Story

Gintoki is conscripted to fight in a feudal war. While awaiting his return, his mother Yone and his wife Shige are raped and killed by a band of passing *samurai*. A black cat wanders into the burnt-out ruins of their home and laps at the faces of their corpses, causing them to return from the dead as vampiric cat spirits. Cursed to now take revenge on all *samurai*, the women lure several into a spooky bamboo grove before tearing their throats out. When Gintoki returns from the war, he is ordered by his cowardly commander Mikado to destroy the spirits, while they become tragically torn between their vengeful impulses and the love they still feel for their son and husband.

Background

Partly based on a Japanese folktale called *The Cat's Revenge*, Shindo's film is probably the definitive entry in the *bakeneko* ('cat demon') subgenre of Japanese horror cinema, which also includes Kunio Watanabe's *Ghost Cat of Nabeshime* (1949), Ryohei Arai's *Ghost Cat of Arima Palace* (1953), Nakagawa's *The Mansion of the Ghost Cat* (1958), and Yoshiro Ishikawa's *The Ghost Cat of Otama Pond* (1960). Japanese theatrical traditions are very much to the fore in this classic *kaidan eiga*, with strong *Noh* elements in some of the staging and choreography, as well as a clear *Kabuki* influence on the aerial acrobatics of the cat spirits.

Verdict

Watching Shindo's *Kuroneko* alongside his *Onibaba* shows just how versatile this director could be. There is the same winning combination of eroticism and brutality, but while his earlier film was primarily a realistic depiction of human savagery, here much of the action plays out like a waking dream. Admittedly, the pair of cat women here are not portrayed with the same subtlety as the feline seductress in Val Lewton's *Cat People* (1942), but Shindo still uses plenty of imaginative touches: we catch glimpses of hair on Shige's arm and her hair swishing like a cat's tail, while Yone laps thirstily at the contents of a cauldron. The house in the bamboo grove that the ghosts reside in has the same eerie atmosphere as spooky Kutsuki Manor in *Tales of Ugetsu*, while the sequences in which the spirits leap gracefully through the air have a haunting beauty – even if the wire work isn't exactly on a par with that of *Crouching Tiger, Hidden Dragon* (2003). There are still moments of pure horror in here, though – it's blood-curdling to watch these creatures fall greedily on the throats of their hapless prey. What catches the viewer most off guard is perhaps the story's romance and pathos – the supernatural nature of the feline ghosts means they must ultimately choose to sacrifice themselves or risk destroying someone they love, making their dilemma rather moving. Those who like a touch of Freud in their films will have plenty to pick through here, too, in the climactic clash between mother and son, as well as the enigmatic final image, which suggests another ghostly rebirth.

SOCIAL SICKNESSES

"Japanese horror movies have the cunning beauty of certain corpses. Sometimes one is stunned by so much cruelty. One seeks its sources in the Asian people's long familiarity with suffering, that requires that even pain be ornate."

Chris Marker's *Sans Soleil* (1983)

The tradition of classic ghost stories was certainly a rich source for post-war Japanese horror, and the *kaidan eiga* certainly still exert a strong influence on contemporary horror films across Asia. But there were other strains of Japanese horror, developed since the sixties, which have also helped shape the modern cinematic landscape – strains which took elements of home-grown and western exploitation, pornography, cyberpunk, urban legends, avant-garde art and comic strips and combined them into some truly heady horrors.

ERO-GRO AND ENTRAILS: JAPANESE EXPLOITATION

Kabuki plays had often featured scenes of torture and cruelty and, following the graphic tableaux of infernal torments at the close of Nakagawa's *Hell* in 1960, a strain of Japanese horror cinema made the unflinching depiction of bodily torments its primary *raison d'être*. Teruo Ishii's anthology film *Joys of Torture* (1968) was the first of a series of eight *Torture* films he would go on to make for Toei Studios over the next five years, many shamelessly using spurious period settings to justify their unremittingly unpleasant depictions of women (and very occasionally men) being tortured. Beheadings, burnings, crucifixions, dismemberments by oxen, bloody tattoos, red-hot pokers and chilli peppers are just some of the punishments we see administered.

Like Toei, Nikkatsu – the oldest Japanese film studio – diversified into pure exploitation territory during the sixties and seventies. Nikkatsu came to be identified primarily with the *pinku eiga* genre, outings in (often fetishistic) soft-core pornography which sometimes incorporated strong elements of violence and horror. Erotic ghost stories were part of *pinku*'s legacy – Chusei Sone's *Hellish Love* (1972) was an explicit revamp of the classic folktale *The Peony Lantern*, first filmed in 1921. Other *pinkus* – like Masumura's *Blind Beast* (1969) and Ishii's *Horrors of Malformed Men* (1969), both Edogawa Rampo adaptations – purveyed a delirious blend of eroticism and grotesque violence known as '*ero-gro*', a style that has been enjoying something of a revival in recent years (see 2005's *Rampo Noir* anthology or Takashi Miike's 2006 *Masters of Horror* offering, *Imprint*).

The 1980s saw a rash of brazen fusions of the *pinku eiga* and the slasher film, often with supernatural twists. Toshiharu Ikeda's *Evil Dead Trap* (1988) was undoubtedly the most impressive of these, while *Notorious Entrails of a Virgin* (1986) and *Entrails of a Beauty* (1986), both directed by Kazuo 'Gaira' Komizu, were also popular. The first of this pairing boasts decapitations, bludgeonings, and the edifying spectacle of a woman masturbating with a severed arm before being disembowelled by a swamp monster sporting a hugely engorged member. Deservedly the most notorious of the 1980s splatter films were the six-part *Guinea Pig* series, kicked off by *Guinea Pig: Devil's Experiment* (1984); hard to justify on any aesthetic level, this virtually unwatchable ultra-low-budget video series largely dispensed with plotting and characterisation in favour of wall-to-wall gore, torture and sexual violence. The second film in the series, Hideshi Hino's *Flowers of Flesh and Blood* (1985), was infamously referred to the MPAA by Hollywood actor Charlie Sheen, who had mistaken it for an actual snuff movie.

Some of the extreme imagery favoured by Japanese exploitation cinema took on fascinating new forms in the nineties, when cyberpunk films harnessed explicit images of sex and violence for more cerebral ends. Shinya Tsukamoto's brace of *Tetsuo* films and his *A Snake of June* took their cues from the two Davids, Lynch and Cronenberg, raising the bar for body horror in their fascination with organic and mechanical hybrids. Kei Fujiwara, one of *Tetsuo*'s stars, made her own intriguing contribution to the genre with *Organ* (1996), a film rife with imagery of phantasmagoric bodily transformations. Special effects maestro Yoshihiro Nishimura followed up his work on sci-fi horror *Meatball Machine* (2005) and *The Machine Girl* (2008) with the dementedly OTT cult cyberpunk film *Tokyo Gore Police* (2008). *Splatter: Naked Blood* (1996), with its grotesque scenes of auto-cannibalism, positioned itself at perhaps the most extreme fringe of extreme cinema: a spectacular collision of art house and grind house – once seen never forgotten.

GHOSTS IN THE MACHINES

Japanese cyberpunk films had their origins in the country's frantic rate of industrialisation as the twentieth century raced to its close, and they reveal profound anxieties about the way technology encroaches on all aspects of modern living. This would become a dominant theme of modern Japanese horror. *Ring*, of course, bequeathed us its famous 'video curse', influencing a whole spate of pan-Asian horror films with plots grounded in haunted technology: Kiyoshi Kurosawa's *Pulse* (2001) featured ghosts infiltrating Internet chat rooms; Korean hit *Phone* (2002) featured a mobile phone serving as a conduit for a vengeful ghost; victims in Takashi Miike's *One Missed Call* (2003) receive phone calls playing the sounds of their own deaths; Ten Shimoyama's *St John's Wort* (2000) features a videogame seeping into reality; and Thai shocker *Shutter* (2004) had a ghost appearing in photos. In all likelihood, these films resonate particularly well with eastern audiences because of the residual influence of animistic religious traditions.

As well as fears about technological developments themselves (the root of the country's prosperity in the post-war boom years), Japanese horror films began to reflect deep unease about their socially isolating effects on users – which have been linked to the high suicide rate among the country's youth. As well as *Pulse*, Shion Sono's *Suicide Circle* (2002) and its imitators *Suicide Manual* (2003) and *Suicide Manual 2: Intermediate Stage* (2003) all present suicide as a kind of 'death-style' trend among alienated youth, and a symptom of an atomised culture that has become so desensitised through technology and modernisation – and so estranged from its traditional Shinto-sanctioned value systems – that it has begun to messily disintegrate. The six films in the *All Night Long* series, directed by Katsuya Matsumura, featured delinquent vigilantes, while *Battle Royale* and its sequel *Battle Royale II: Requiem* (2003) were prominent (and keenly discussed) contributions to this trend in dystopian horror, reflecting fears of social collapse in the wake of the bursting of Japan's economic bubble in the nineties. Social breakdown – like the passing around of the videotapes in *Ring* – has a contagious, viral quality that is reflected in much Japanese horror: in Takeshi Kawamura's *Last Frankenstein* (1992), a virus causes characters to commit suicide years after their first exposure.

As we saw in the previous chapter, much Japanese horror since World War Two had been fuelled by fears of what the forces of modernisation and westernisation were doing to a culture founded on conservative traditional values, and the economic recession of the nineties brought some of these issues into sharp relief. Increased unemployment and job insecurity produced a rise in domestic violence, and the nuclear family (which had replaced the extended traditional family structures of the pre-World War Two period) became increasingly fragile. *Ring* and *Dark Water* feature single working mothers and neglected children, while the entire backstory of *Ju-On:*

42

The Grudge is fuelled by the murderous anger of a man towards his wife and child. Few films have skewered the gnawing unease caused by changing gender roles as adroitly as Miike's *Audition* (1999), whose protagonist's complacent assumptions about the passivity of his partner prove hideously unfounded, while the same director's wildly subversive V-Cinema effort *Visitor Q* (2001) is a jaw-dropping satire on a nuclear family that spectacularly implodes in a riot of excrement, anal rape and breast milk.

JAPANESE V-CINEMA AND NORIO TSURUTA

Actually a Toei trademark, 'V-Cinema' has become the western designation since the 1980s for direct-to-video Japanese releases (known locally as 'OV' or 'Original Video'), an important outlet for horror. These releases may be low budget, but they can carry more kudos than their equivalents in the west (nauseating *Guinea Pig* films notwithstanding), as well as being exempt from the same censorship restrictions as cinema releases. Takashi Shimizu's first pair of *Ju-On: The Curse* films were made as V-Cinema projects, Kiyoshi Kurosawa delivered V-Cinema pieces like *Door III* (1996) in between more prestigious theatrical releases, and Takashi Miike still sporadically returns to plough the V-Cinema furrow (the outrageous *Theorem* [1968] parody *Visitor Q* was made after the success of *Audition* as part of a six-film project called *LoveCinema*).

One of the key V-Cinema horror specialists was Norio Tsuruta, who, in the early nineties, made three groundbreaking volumes of a contemporary *kaidan* series called *Scary True Stories* (1992), which had a significant influence on the J-Horror wave that was to break later in the decade. The incidents depicted in the films were all based on real-life testimony (each begins with a photo of the individuals involved), and many featured black-haired *yurei*. Through their atmospheric camera and lighting styles and their creative use of unnerving sound effects, these *Stories* set the template for the visual and aural style of films like *Ring* and *Ju-On: The Grudge*, and Hideo Nakata cut his own directing teeth on a trio of episodes later known as *Curse, Death & Spirit*. Tsuruta himself would later find a place on the fringes of the big league, directing *Ring 0: Birthday* (2000), the *Wicker Man*-influenced Junji Ito *manga* adaptation *Scarecrow* (2001) and *Premonition* (2004), the second instalment of producer Taka Ichise's *J-Horror Theatre* series. Like Miike, Tsuruta has also directed an entry in the American *Masters of Horror* series (*Dream Cruise*), based on a short story by *Ring* author Koji Suzuki.

WESTERN HORRORS, JAPANESE STYLE

Ever alert to international trends, Japanese horror producers have always been quick to devise their own variations on American and European horror hits. Shohei Imamura had directed the impressive serial-killer thriller *Vengeance is Mine* in 1979, based on the police hunt for the real-life serial killer Akira Nishiguchi, and Koji Wakamatsu's violent *Violated Angels* (1967), an example of *ero-gro*, had been based on the exploits of the Chicago rapist-murderer Richard Speck, but the success of *Silence of the Lambs* (1991) and *Se7en* in the nineties created a fresh vogue for psycho thrillers. Some commentators have noted serial killers in Japanese movies are often immersed in *otaku* culture – the realm of lonely, obsessive anorak males hiding behind the protective barriers of technology and preferring virtual relationships to real ones. Ataru Oikawa's *Tokyo Psycho* (2004) was loosely based on the case of Miyazaki Tsutomu, the horrific '*Otaku* murderer' of the late eighties who mutilated and murdered four very young girls.

Japanese serial-killer flicks often delivered interesting twists on their western counterparts. Kiyoshi Kurosawa's *The Guard from the Underground* (1992) featured a sumo wrestler-turned-security guard as its murderer, while his splendid *Cure* (1997) featured a deranged mesmerist. The Clarice Starling-esque heroine of Sogo Ishii's *Angel*

Dust (1994) gets into such a headspin that she starts to believe that she herself is a prolific poison-needle murderess. Another intriguing Japanese contribution to the genre was Joji Iida's *Another Heaven* (2000), which featured a body-hopping serial killer stalking Tokyo after having grown bored of the afterlife. Although influenced by the supernatural entities of American films like Jack Sholder's *The Hidden* (1988) and Gregory Hoblit's *Fallen* (1998), Iida's brain-munching creature has a few memorable tricks of his own: an early sequence has the police discovering its first victim with his head sliced open and his grey matter stewing on the stove.

Other western horror staples have been creatively reworked by Japanese filmmakers in recent years. Takashi Ishii's *Freeze Me* (2000) was a rape-revenge thriller in the vein of Meir Zarchi's *I Spit On Your Grave* (1978) or Abel Ferrara's *Ms. 45* (1981), whose heroine avenges herself by murdering the men who raped her before putting their corpses on ice in industrial freezers, while Miike's *Audition* cleverly toyed with the theme of a scorned and violated woman turning the tables on her tormentors. George Romero's seminal *Dead* films were a clear influence on the spate of Japanese zombie movies that have surfaced in the last decade (the success of the Romero-esque *Resident Evil* computer games doubtless providing the green light). Kitamura's *Versus* (2000) was a frenzied yakuza/ zombie/martial arts mash-up that wore its Sam Raimi and Peter Jackson borrowings proudly on its sleeve, while Tetsuro Takeuchi's *Wild Zero* (2000) was a sporadically entertaining, self-consciously cultish, rock 'n' roll zombie sci-fi comedy showcasing Japanese band Guitar Wolf. Just as they created Godzilla, the US military were behind the zombie outbreak in Atsushi Muroga's *Junk: Evil Dead Hunting* (2000), while in Sakichi Sato's parodic *Tokyo Zombie* (2005) creatures are revived from the dead by toxic waste from the mounds of refuse generated by Tokyo's complacent citizens. The voracious zombie schoolgirls of Naoyuki Tomomatsu's *Stacy* (2001) have been perhaps the most entertaining recent twist on the genre.

The nineties had, in fact, seen a major rise in horror targeted at teenage audiences. Shimako Sato's *Eko Eko Azarak: Wizard of Darkness* (1995) was conceived very much in the spirit of *Buffy the Vampire Slayer* (1992), and was enough of a runaway hit to spawn five sequels. Earlier in the decade, Norio Tsuruta's *Scary True Stories* TV series (1992) had paved the way for the successful *Haunted School* TV mini-series dramatising the creepy urban legends spread by schoolchildren; both series sowed the seeds for *Ring*'s success. More recently, goremeister Yoshihiro Nishimura's ultra-parodic *Vampire Girl vs Frankenstein Girl* (2009) has proved that a sexy slice of high-school horror is still a sure way to win over a hormonal, pubescent audience.

MANGA AND ANIME

Japanese *manga* has been an increasingly important source for cinematic horrors in recent years, and many key works – including *Uzumaki* (2000), *Tomie* (2001), *Premonition*, the *Death Note* films (2006–8), *Ichi the Killer* (2001), the *MPD Psycho* TV series (2000) and even the Korean *Old Boy* (2003) – are based on comic strips. The hallmarks of many of these works are outrageous visual conceits, ripped straight from the pages of their sources: the villagers in *Uzumaki* are taken over by an obsession with spirals that contorts their bodies into hallucinatory shapes; *Death Note*'s protagonist is taken under the bat-wing of a smirking, apple-eating CGI demon with filed teeth and a taste for vintage Goth apparel; and Miike's infamous *Ichi* features a superhero suit customised with retractable razor-sharp blades that slice people in half, a man tortured by being dangled from fish hooks and scalded with hot oil pooled in the small of his back, and a flamboyantly psychotic villain with a grotesque gash for a mouth, pinned into place at the sides.

Anime has been written about extensively in more specialist studies, and falls largely outside of the scope of this book. Suffice to say that many Japanese animated horror films engage with the same themes as live-action ones. *Serial Experiments: Lain* (1998) tackles similar themes to Kurosawa's *Pulse*, while the creepy *Perfect Blue* (1998) is regarded as a superior specimen of psycho-thriller. *Vampire Hunter D* (1985) is an ultra-gory tale in the style of the American *Blade* comics and films about a half-human, half-vampire antihero battling a vampire Count, while the stylish *Blood: The Last Vampire* (2000) shared a similar premise (the latter was transformed into an ambitious live-action version in 2009). The *manga* adaptation *Urotsukidoji* (1987) and its sequels attracted plenty of international notoriety by popularising the *shokushu goukan* ('tentacle rape') subgenre in which women are penetrated by monstrous demonic appendages – a tradition going back to Edo-era *Ukiyo-e* woodcuts by Hokusai, revived to circumvent modern-day censorship restrictions on depicting penises (tentacles and robotic substitutes are, apparently, acceptable).

JAPANESE MODERN HORROR MASTERS: THE BIG FIVE

HIDEO NAKATA

Nakata's *Ring* kick-started the J-Horror boom, even though he himself has expressed a certain disdain for the horror genre ('Horror isn't my natural genre, but I've learned it as a directing skill,' he has commented). Born in 1961 in Okayama, Nakata trained in journalism at the University of Tokyo before being taken on as an assistant director on *pinku eiga* at Nikkatsu Studios. He cut his teeth directing a trio of spooky shorts, subsequently known as *Curse, Death & Spirit* (1992), which formed part of Norio Tsuruta's *Scary True Stories* series (see above). Each story is introduced as an event experienced by a real person. *A Cursed Doll* is about a young girl terrorised by the titular toy, which is possessed by the restless spirit of her dead sister, while *Waterfall of the Dead Spirit*, featuring a ghost woman trying to keep a young boy bound to her forever in her watery lair, is an interesting precursor to the themes of Nakata's later *Dark Water*. The third piece, *An Inn Where a Ghost Lives*, features three young girls armed with a video camera who check into a haunted house and encounter an archetypal long-haired, white-robed, staring-eyed *yurei*. While these early works – shot on video – have limited production values and don't deliver the expert hair-raising scares that would later make Nakata's name, they provide an interesting foretaste of his future landmark works.

His first solo feature assignment was the made-for-TV *God's Hand* (1992), written by Hiroshi Takahashi (*Ring*'s future screenwriter). It was his follow-up, *Ghost Actress* (1996), a tale of a haunted film set also scripted by Takahashi, which brought him to the attention of *Ring* author Koji Suzuki. The huge success of his adaptation led directly to the proficient sequel *Ring 2*, after which Nakata changed tack by directing the teen romance *Sleeping Bride* (2000) and his most undervalued work, *Chaos* (2000), a *Vertigo*-inspired psychological thriller based on a novel by Shogo Utani. Despite its weak, throwaway ending, the film is an intriguing portrayal of the sado-masochistic relationship that develops between a woman and the man she hires to kidnap her, and builds up a satisfyingly tangled web of deceit, double-cross and murder for the viewer to unpick. It allowed Nakata to stretch his directing muscles with a project filmed largely on location rather than within the confines of studio sets. *Dark Water* (2002) remains the director's masterpiece – one of the undisputed highlights of the J-Horror cycle. With *The Ring Two* (2005), Nakata gained the distinction of making his Hollywood debut with a sequel to a remake of his own film. More recently, Nakata has directed *Kaidan* (an adaptation of an 1860s *kaidan* about the doomed lovers of the Kasane swamp, also filmed by Mizoguchi and Nakagawa) and *L: Change the World*, a spin-off of the phenomenally popular *Death Note* film. He is rumoured to now be prepping a bio-pic of *Kwaidan* author Lafcadio Hearn, and is attached as director of *The Ring Three*.

Key Horror Works

Curse, Death & Spirit (1992), *Ghost Actress* (1996), *Haunted School F* (1997, co-directed with Kiyoshi Kurosawa), *Ring* (1998), *Ring 2* (1999), *Chaos* (2000), *Dark Water* (2002), *The Ring Two* (2005), *Kaidan* (2007), *L: Change the World* (2007)

KIYOSHI KUROSAWA

Born in Kobe in 1955, the prolific and versatile Kurosawa (no relation to the great Akira) cut his teeth in the 1980s on a plethora of Super-8 shorts, V-Cinema *yakuza* pics and *pinku* projects for Nikkatsu. His haunted-house film *Sweet Home* (1989), produced by the celebrated director Juzo Itami (*Tampopo* [1985], *A Taxing Woman* [1987]), was a *Poltergeist* (1982) variant boasting makeup effects by Hollywood maestro Dick Smith (*The Exorcist*, 1973). Kurosawa ended up suing Itami after the producer re-shot and re-edited parts of the film for video and TV release, temporarily making him *persona non grata* in the Japanese film industry.

After a spell directing TV horror pieces (including a stint on Kansai's anthology series *Haunted School*, 1994), he won himself a scholarship to Robert Redford's Sundance Institute in the early nineties. Kurosawa returned to the fray with the violent slasher *The Guard from the Underground* (1992), in which a psychotic security guard slaughters a group of employees trapped overnight in his office building. But it was the ambitious, highly accomplished *Cure* (1997) that proved to be Kurosawa's real breakthrough – a *Se7en*-influenced serial-killer thriller in which a policeman discovers that a spate of seemingly unconnected murders have been engineered by a sociopathic mesmerist. *Charisma* (1999), based on the script that won him his Sundance place, was a bizarre, curiously poetic, allegorical oddity about an eponymous toxic tree with the potential to destroy the world. He unleashed his landmark apocalyptic horror fable *Pulse* in 2001, preceded by the TV movie *Séance* (2000) in which a couple are haunted by the ghost of a child they never had. *Bright Future* (2003) – an existential parable featuring poisonous jellyfish – and *Doppelganger* (2003) confirmed Kurosawa's status as one of the country's most distinctive auteurs and the leading light of Japanese cinema's cerebral, Godard-influenced 'New New Wave'. The J-Horror haunted-house film *Loft* (2005) followed, in which a writer's vacation in a country house is plagued by various unquiet spirits, along with *Retribution* (2006) – a film originally intended as part of producer Taka Ichise's J-Horror Theatre series – which featured a detective haunted by a ghost while investigating a murder in which he himself seems to be implicated. A hard man to pigeon-hole, Kurosawa's meditative *Tokyo Sonata* – touted as a Japanese variant on *Bicycle Thieves* (1948) – bagged him the Un Certain Regard Jury Prize at the 2008 Cannes Film Festival.

Key Horror Works

Sweet Home (1989), *The Guard from the Underground* (1992), *Haunted School* (TV, 1994), *Door III* (1996), *Haunted School F* (1997, co-directed with Hideo Nakata), *Cure* (1997), *Charisma* (1999), *Pulse* (2001), *Bright Future* (2003), *Doppelganger* (2003), *Loft* (2005), *Retribution* (2006)

SHINYA TSUKAMOTO

Born in Tokyo in 1960, Tsukamoto made numerous Super-8 pieces as a teenager, before enrolling in the Fine Arts Department of Nihon University. After graduating in 1982, he did a stint in advertising before forming Tokyo's experimental Kaiju Theatre Group in 1986. One of their innovative productions was *The Adventures of Electric Rod Boy* (aka *The Great Analog World*), which they decided to make a Super-8 film version of after its initial staging. It concerned a boy (with an electricity pylon sprouting from his back) transported to the future to defeat a horde of cyborg vampires plotting to eradicate sunlight. His cyberpunk classic *Tetsuo: The Iron Man* (1988) was shot on black-and-white 16mm with several of his Kaiju collaborators and became an international cult hit. Tsukamoto followed this up with the more commercial, major-studio horror *Hiruko the Goblin* (1990), about a boy hunting down the demon who has stolen his girlfriend's head, before reworking the original *Tetsuo* as *Tetsuo II: Body Hammer* (1992) in 35mm colour. He then broadened his palette with the boxing drama *Tokyo Fist* (1995) which – exaggerated bloodletting aside – was in a more realist vein, while *Bullet Ballet* (1998) saw him striking out confidently into *film noir* territory. *Gemini* (1999) was an impressive adaptation of an Edogawa Rampo story in which a young doctor's comfortable life is overturned by a malevolent doppelganger who imprisons him in a well and shacks up with his amnesiac wife. Bizarre love triangles were also to the fore in his next two films: *A Snake of June* (2002) featured a woman blackmailed into performing exhibitionist sex acts, while *Vital* (2004) involved an amnesiac medical student dissecting the corpse of his girlfriend. After the short *Haze* (2005) came the impressive and domestically successful *Nightmare Detective* (2006), involving the hunt for 'Zero', a Freddy Krueger-style serial killer (played by Tsukamoto himself) who can enter his victims' dreams; Tsukamoto is notching up further instalments to make up a trilogy. Tsukamoto often acts in his own films and frequently takes roles in other directors' work – including Miike's *Ichi the Killer* and Shimizu's *Marebito*. Many of his films are memorably scored by Japanese industrial 'Metal Percussion' specialists Der Eisenrost.

Key Horror Works

Tetsuo: The Iron Man (1988), *Hiruko the Goblin* (1990), *Tetsuo II: Body Hammer* (1992), *Gemini* (1999), *A Snake of June* (2002), *Vital* (2004), *Haze* (2005), *Nightmare Detective* (2006), *Nightmare Detective 2* (2008), *Tetsuo: The Bullet Man* (2010)

TAKASHI MIIKE

Invariably sporting a rakish pair of sunglasses in public (and very probably in private too), Miike seems to revel in his reputation as the undisputed *enfant terrible* of modern Japanese cinema – a provocative *shockmeister* intent on transgressing all boundaries of taste and propriety. And yet, even though several of his films certainly warrant their notoriety, they constitute a relatively small sampling of his overall output, which is massively prolific and surprisingly varied. For every *Ichi the Killer* or *Visitor Q*, there are the more tender and restrained narratives of *Rainy Dog* (1997) or *The Bird People in China* (1998) to consider.

Born in 1960 in Osaka, Miike graduated from the Yokohama Vocational School of Broadcast and Film under the guidance of the institution's founder, renowned director Shohei Imamura. Miike went on to work as an assistant director on several films (including Imamura's 1989 *Black Rain*) before getting swept up in the V-Cinema boom of the early nineties and becoming a director himself. After developing a reputation as a *yakuza* specialist, he made his theatrical debut with *Shinjuku Triad Society* (1995), although it was the following year's violent, hyperbolic *manga* adaptation, *Fudoh: The New Generation*, that caused ripples on the international festival circuit. But it was, of course, the shockwaves of *Audition* (1999) that really put Miike on the map, marking (alongside *Ring*) the resurgence of Asian horror in the West. The satirical, taboo-busting *Visitor Q* (2001) – featuring anal rape, incest, necrophilia and copious amounts of lactation – and the ultra-violent *Ichi the Killer* (2001) further cemented Miike's reputation as a purveyor of outrageous excess.

Miike's filmography contains relatively few examples of 'pure' horror. His most mainstream film to date has been *One Missed Call* (2003), a domestic J-Horror smash (based on a novel by Yasushi Akimoto) featuring inventive death scenes and owing a substantial debt to *Ring* (mobile-phone messages relay the sound of the listener's imminent death). His English-language debut, an entry in Showtime's US *Masters of Horror* series entitled *Imprint* (2006), had the distinction of being deemed too disturbing for Stateside broadcast (it was later released on DVD). Based on a novel by Shimako Iwai and set in the nineteenth century, it featured Billy Drago as an American journalist visiting an island brothel to track down an old flame, where he is told a set of *Rashomon*-style conflicting stories about how she may have been framed for theft and subsequently driven to suicide. A work squarely in the *ero-gro* tradition, *Imprint* featured nauseating scenes of protracted torture, in which a woman is strung up and mutilated, as well as a parasitic mutant sibling lifted from *Evil Dead Trap* (1988). *Box*, Miike's earlier contribution to the pan-Asian anthology film *Three... Extremes* (2004), was a more subtly satisfying offering in which a writer is plagued by guilty nightmares stemming from a horrific childhood accident in which her sister was burned alive while they were rehearsing a circus act.

Elsewhere, Miike has gleefully welded horror tropes to other genres to startling effect. *The Happiness of the Katakuris* (2001), a loose remake of Ji-woon Kim's horror-comedy *The Quiet Family* (1998), is a highly entertaining, one-of-a-kind, genre-busting zombie musical. Also notable is his six-part TV series *MPD Psycho* (2000), adapted by Miike himself from Eiji Otsuka's labyrinthine *manga*. Featuring a detective suffering from the titular Multiple Personality Disorder tracking down a cult leader responsible for a series of gruesome deaths, the series incorporates numerous surreal touches (the victims all have a barcode tattoo) and flurries of stomach-flipping gore into its police-procedural framework. *The Great Yokai War* (2005) was a fantasy-horror kids' film, dense with CGI and stop-motion puppetry, about a young boy battling an evil *Dracula*-esque spirit hell-bent on creating an army of servile monsters out of piles of waste.

Key Horror Works

Audition (1999), *MPD Psycho* (TV, 2000), *Visitor Q* (2001), *Ichi the Killer* (2001), *The Happiness of the Katakuris* (2001), *One Missed Call* (2003), *Box* (2004), *The Great Yokai War* (2005), *Imprint* (2006)

TAKASHI SHIMIZU

Shimizu remains best known for his seemingly never-ending work on the expanding *Ju-On* franchise, which he has straddled like a colossus. Born in 1972 in Maebashi City, Shimizu was a graduate of the Tokyo Film Seminar (later the Film School of Tokyo), where he benefited from the tutelage of Kiyoshi Kurosawa and *Ring* scriptwriter Hiroshi Takahashi. Shimizu's first professional gig came courtesy of Kurosawa, who put him forward to direct a pair of segments of *Haunted School G* for Kansai TV, which he then expanded in 2000 into the V-Cinema films *Ju-On: The Curse* and *Ju-On: The Curse 2*. He then directed *Ju-On: The Grudge* (2002) – still a strong contender for the all-time-scariest J-Horror film. He followed this up with the almost equally frightening *Ju-On: The Grudge 2* (2003), before heading to Hollywood to helm *The Grudge* (2004) and *The Grudge 2* (2006). In between these instalments, he also made his debut theatrical feature, *Tomie: Rebirth* (2001), the best of the numerous adaptations of Junji Ito's popular *manga* series about the vengeful spirit of a dismembered schoolgirl, the fascinating *Marebito* (2004), the *Blonde Kwaidan* episode of the portmanteau *Dark Tales of Japan* (2004) and *Reincarnation* (2005), the third instalment of the J-Horror Theatre Series. Shimizu has admitted to being strongly influenced by US horror films like *A Nightmare on Elm Street* (1984), *Evil Dead* (1981) and – in particular – *The Shining* (1980).

Key Horror Works

Ju-On: The Curse (2000), *Ju-On: The Curse 2* (2000), *Tomie: Rebirth* (2001), *Ju-On: The Grudge* (2002), *Ju-On: The Grudge 2* (2003), *Marebito* (aka *The Stranger from Afar*, 2004), *The Grudge* (2004), *Blonde Kwaidan* (2004), *Reincarnation* (2005), *The Grudge 2* (2006)

MODERN JAPANESE HORROR: ESSENTIAL VIEWING

Blind Beast/ Moju (1969)

Directed by: Yasuzo Masumura
Cast: Eiji Funakoshi (Michio), Mako Midori (Aki), Noriko Sengoku (Mother)

Story

Michio, a psychopathic, blind sculptor, kidnaps beautiful model Aki and locks her up in his warehouse studio under the guard of his overbearing mother. Michio wants to use his prisoner to create a new genre of art. Artist and model subject each other to a series of sado-masochistic mind and body games, involving murder, rape and – eventually – love. As her affection for Michio deepens, Aki starts to go blind herself, and they begin to explore the limits of sensation by biting, clawing, beating and whipping each other, before pushing their bizarre love affair to even more perverse extremes.

Background

This film remains one of the most fascinating examples of the first wave of *pinku eiga* that ran from 1964 until 1972. Masumura's other works include the lesbian melodrama *Manji* (1964) and the frontline nursing saga *Red Angel* (1966). In his disdain for the cosy conservatism of mainstream Japanese cinema, he was a big influence on other

Japanese New Wave directors of the sixties – including Shohei Imamura and Nagisa Oshima, whose *In the Realm of the Senses* (1976) owes a significant debt to *Blind Beast* (and to its outrageous finale, in particular). This film was based on a story by Edogawa Rampo that was first serialised in the *Asahi* national newspaper in the early 1930s. Rampo's writings have been adapted into other notable horrors like *The Palette Knife Murder* (1946), Kinji Fukasaku's *Black Lizard* (1968), Teruo Ishii's *Horrors of Malformed Men* (1969), Noboru Tanaka's *Watcher in the Attic* (1976), Shinya Tsukamoto's *Gemini* (1999) and the portmanteau *Rampo Noir* (2005), while the man himself was given an unorthodox biopic treatment in 1994's bizarre *Rampo*.

Verdict

This exceptionally lurid blend of horror and sexploitation really has to be seen to be (dis)believed, and those wanting to sample the occasionally dubious but frequently inspired delights of *ero-gro* should start here. Laughing in the face of any notion of political correctness, Masumura's film – like Cronenberg's *Crash* (1996) many years later – explores the outer fringes of sexual ecstasy, where desire mutates into something deeply destructive, curiously beautiful and altogether new. Heavily Freudian, much of the action is set in artist Michio's jaw-dropping warehouse studio – a surreal dreamscape of giant body sculptures and clusters of oversized body parts protruding from the walls. At one point, the heroine, Aki, realises that the enormity of the body parts is based on her captor's vision of the world as a baby, before the onset of his blindness. Michio, a teetotal virgin, literally ends up destroying his mother in order to progress to the next stage of his deeply perverse sexual development. In its depiction of a twisted romance that goes well and truly off the rails, *Blind Beast* anticipates Miike's *Audition*, while, as *Rampo Noir* (2005) has recently demonstrated, the writer's brand of hallucinogenic horror is once again in vogue.

Evil Dead Trap/Shiryo no Wana (1988)

Directed by: Toshiharu Ikeda
Cast: Miyuki Ono (Nami), Aya Katsuragi (Masako Abe), Hitomi Kobayashi (Rei Sugiura), Yuji Honma (Muraki)

Story

TV host Nami is sent a videotape showing the torture and killing of a young woman. The tape also reveals directions to a disused army base, where Nami promptly heads with four members of her production team to investigate. They meet an enigmatic individual who claims to have grown up on the base with his disturbed brother, Hideki. A sinister figure in a raincoat starts killing off each member of the team in gruesomely extreme ways, until only Nami remains to learn the shocking truth about the monstrous Hideki.

Background

Japan Home Video stumped up the money for Nikkatsu Studios veteran and *pinku* specialist Ikeda to make this modern exploitation classic, and were keen to showcase the talents of a pair of the adult movie actresses in their stable – hence the inclusion in the film of a couple of steamy sex scenes just before the slice-and-dice gets underway in earnest. The film's screenwriter, Takashi Ishii, was a former *manga* artist, and would go on to become a respected director with the *yakuza* thriller *Gonin* (1995) and the rape-revenge saga *Freeze Me* (2000). Two inferior sequels, the first made without the involvement of Ikeda and Ishii, followed over the next five years. Ikeda made several erotic thrillers and *yakuza* films in the nineties, before returning to the horror genre with the teen-*manga* adaptation *Shadow of the Wraith* in 2004 and the playful serial-killer pastiche *The Man Behind the Scissors* (2004).

Verdict

This superior slasher is a great example of the ways in which eastern and western horror films have always fed off and renewed each other in a mutually beneficial cycle. Ikeda's film harks back to American classics like *The Texas Chain Saw Massacre* (1974) and *The Evil Dead*, but its biggest debt is to the baroque Italian *giallo* thrillers of Dario Argento (*Deep Red* [1975], *Suspiria* [1977], *Tenebrae* [1982]). Tomohiko Kira's synthesised score is a direct lift from the soundtracks produced by Goblin for Argento's films, while the highly stylised, expressionist lighting and the gory *coups de grâce* delivered to the comely female characters are very much the Italian maestro's *modus operandi*. Not content, though, with having a killer who is merely psychotic, Ikeda and Ishii up the ante in the final reel and throw in a dose of demented Cronenbergian body horror for good measure. Splatter hounds have a host of creatively executed gougings, garrottings, impalements and decapitations to enjoy, while the slick pacing, clever visuals, entertaining psychobabble ('Mama-freak, or split personality?,' Nami asks the putative murderer) and comic-book garishness of the whole enterprise are also to savour.

Tetsuo: The Iron Man (1988)

Directed by: Shinya Tsukamoto
Cast: Shinya Tsukamoto (Metal Fetishist), Tomorowo Taguchi (Man), Kei Fujiwara (Woman)

Story

A Tokyo salaryman kills a metal fetishist in a hit-and-run incident. The salaryman is pursued through the subway by a woman whose body has been taken over by the fetishist. The salaryman's own body begins to mutate into a flesh and metal hybrid. Unable to control his transformation, he ends up killing his girlfriend with a drill formed from his mutated penis. The salaryman then engages in a protracted and violent homoerotic duel with the fetishist.

Background

This was Tsukamoto's first 16mm film after his earlier 8mm works, and was an international cult hit. His follow-up, *Tetsuo II: Body Hammer*, was actually a bigger-budget 'revisioning' (as was Raimi's *Evil Dead 2* [1987], for example) rather than a direct sequel, while the English-language *Tetsuo: The Bullet Man* (2010) would develop on the original's storyline. *Tetsuo*'s female lead, Kei Fujiwara, did half of the film's cinematography and would go on to direct several features, including the phantasmagorical *Organ* (1996).

Verdict

Tsukamoto's brilliant feature is one of cinema's key works of 'body horror' and leaves an indelible impression on all who see it. A total assault on the senses, the film uses manic pacing, visual distortions, a percussive industrial soundtrack punctuated by grunts and groans, and grotesque, staccato, stop-motion FX sequences of bodies wrenched painfully into monstrous biomechanical hybrids to create a nightmare vision of a society in post-technological meltdown. Incorporating a delirious blend of influences – ranging from cyberpunk, *manga* and Toho's *kaidan eiga* to rock videos, *pinku* misogynist violence, Svankmajer's *Dimensions of Dialogue* (1982), Cronenberg's 'New Flesh' and *Eraserhead*'s (1977) post-industrial monochrome nightmares – this landmark work of Japanese horror is a hysterical articulation of a culture's repressed terror at the technologies it has become enslaved to.

Splatter: Naked Blood/Megyaku: Nekeddo Buraddo (1996)

Directed by: Hisayasu Sato
Cast: Sadao Abe (Eiji), Misa Aika (Rika), Masumi Nakao (Yuki)

Story

Seventeen-year-old boy genius Eiji, while attempting to devise the 'ultimate painkiller' to improve mankind's happiness, creates a new drug called Myson which causes the human brain to experience pain as pleasure. He secretly tests the drug on three young women who are participating in medical contraceptive experiments being run by his mother. One of the women is narcissistic and ends up mutilating herself. Another is gluttonous and starts to slowly eat herself. Eiji is attracted to the third girl, Rika, an insomniac. She introduces him to her 'sleeping installation', a virtual reality unit that allows her to experience dreamlike states by showing the scenery of the heart. Gradually, Eiji begins to comprehend that Myson has transformed Rika into a homicidal sadist.

Background

Sato was one of the major players in the Japanese sex film industry of the eighties and nineties, with over 50 movies under his belt. However, despite the generic constraints he was working under (i.e. a prescribed number of sex scenes), he often had considerable latitude to experiment with form and narrative, leading to the creation of some memorably extreme V-Cinema sex/horror hybrids. *Splatter: Naked Blood* is, in part, a remake of his *pinku eiga* from 1987, *Genuine Rape*, which also explored the boundaries between hallucination and reality. Many of his works were released under impressively lurid titles (samples include *Promiscuous Wife: Disgraceful Torture* [1992] and *S&M Group Wax Torture* [1992]), and some are gratuitously repulsive in their blatant misogyny. Sato later directed the *Caterpillar* segment of the *ero-gro* anthology *Rampo Noir* (2005) and *Tokyo Zombie* (2005).

Verdict

As an example of the 'extreme' fringe of Japanese filmmaking, Sato's notorious splatterpunk/cyberpunk mash-up takes some beating. There had been a tradition of self-mutilation in certain *Kabuki* plays, in which women ritualistically cut off their fingers: Sato takes things to a whole other level when one of his characters dips her hand in boiling fat and proceeds to eat her digits as if they were *tempura* snacks. And that scene turns out to be a mere appetiser for the excruciatingly graphic depictions of corporal consumption to follow. These scenes would be wholly unpalatable if not for the intriguing elements of existential sci-fi that Sato throws into the mix: his film is fixated on virtual realities, altered states, designer drugs and body modification in ways that will endear it to fans of Cronenberg and Philip K Dick. Like other strains of modern Japanese cinema, Sato's film expresses the alienating and isolating effects of modern urban environments, and a gnawing ambivalence about the vaunted benefits of technology.

Ring/Ringu (1998)

Directed by: Hideo Nakata
Cast: Nanako Matsushima (Reiko), Hiroyuki Sanada (Ryuji), Rikiya Otaka (Yoichi)

Story

Tokyo TV journalist Reiko sets out to investigate a series of mysterious deaths caused by a terrifying 'video curse'. Each of the victims who watched a particular videotape received a phone call immediately afterwards informing them they had a week to live. Reiko herself becomes exposed to the curse when she travels to a resort cabin on the Izu peninsula where some of the victims had stayed. Having enlisted the help of her ex-husband Ryuji, they gradually uncover the bizarre history of a psychic woman, Shizuko, who hurled herself into the volcano on Oshima Island 40 years before. They learn that the source of the curse is Shizuko's daughter, Sadako, who was buried alive in a deep well under the Izu cabin by her putative father Dr Ikuma. Reiko and Ryuji race against time to save themselves and their son Yoichi from 'Sadako's fury' by working out how to cancel the curse.

Background

Ring was based on a teen novel published in 1991 by Koji Suzuki (1957–), a writer often referred to as 'the Japanese Stephen King'. The book was a genuine phenomenon on its home turf, selling over 2.5 million copies in Japan alone. It was the first part of a trilogy completed by 1995's *Spiral* and 1998's *Loop*. There had already been a popular, sexed-up TV adaptation of *Ring* on Fuji Television in 1995 before film producer Masato Hara acquired the rights to Suzuki's trilogy and – having decided to shoot adaptations of the first two volumes back to back – hired Nakata to direct *Ring* and Joji Iida to direct *Spiral* (1998). Initially released on a double bill, the former far eclipsed the latter in popularity, becoming a smash hit in Hong Kong and Japan's all-time-highest-grossing horror pic. Nakata and his scriptwriter Hiroshi Takahashi made several key changes to their source, getting rid of the idea of the tape as a literal (smallpox) virus and adding a rich family dynamic by changing the sex of the main character to female.

Following the film's success, Hara asked Nakata and Takahashi to devise a follow-up to *Ring* that could exist as an alternative to the 'official' *Spiral* adaptation, and they promptly delivered the creditable sequel *Ring 2* (1999), which continued to explore Suzuki's concept of a 'psychic virus'. The principal character this time was Ryuji's girlfriend Mai (Miki Nakatani). Norio Tsuruta then made a prequel, *Ring 0: Birthday* (2000), exploring the genesis of Sadako's evil behaviour during her time as a drama student, while die-hard fans of the franchise could also seek out Dong-bin Kim's Korean version *The Ring Virus* (1999), which was actually a slightly more faithful rendering of Suzuki's original *Ring* novel (reinstating Sadako's hermaphroditic nature). Gore Verbinski's Hollywood remake *The Ring* arrived in 2002, followed by its Nakata-helmed sequel in 2005.

Verdict

For today's western audiences, *Ring* is ground zero for any appreciation or exploration of modern Asian horror films, and J-Horror in particular. Its brilliance lies in its canny combination of some of the iconography of classic Japanese horror cinema with modern urban legends and technological fears (mixed with a dash of MR James's cursed-parchment story, *Casting the Runes*, filmed by Jacques Tourneur in 1957 as *Night of the Demon*, for good measure). As such, it manages to play both as an elegant chiller in the *kaidan eiga* tradition and as a post-*Scream*, teen-appeal shocker. Sadako, as should be clear, is merely the modern apotheosis of a long line of theatrical and cinematic *yurei*, glaring balefully from behind their curtain of black hair, while the deep well at the heart of the story echoes back through the pit in *Onibaba* to the classic folktale of samurai Aoyama and his maid Okiku.

Although it contains some of the cinema's most memorable all-time scares (particularly the indelible image of Sadako hauling herself like a broken mannequin out of Ryuji's TV screen), Nakata's real achievement is to dignify his pulpy material with a sense of seriousness. The story is extremely well paced, with the jeopardy neatly notching up as Reiko runs out of time while frantically uncovering the intriguing – if convoluted – backstory of the tragic Shizuko and her malevolent daughter. As in his later *Dark Water*, Nakata generates an eerie, otherworldly atmosphere with the help of subtle lighting effects, a colour scheme awash in dank blues and greens and a creepily discordant soundtrack by Kenji Kawai based on processed industrial noise.

Audition/Odishon (1999)

Directed by: Takashi Miike
Cast: Ryo Ishibashi (Aoyama), Eihi Shiina (Asami), Tetsu Sawaki (Shigehiko), Jun Kunimura (Yoshikawa)

Story

Widower and video producer Aoyama, living with his teenage son, decides to remarry seven years after his wife's death. His friend Yoshikawa suggests that he use a casting session for a fake movie to 'audition' prospective new brides. Aoyama is particularly struck by Asami, a former ballet dancer, and they start dating – despite Yoshikawa's unease. Aoyama takes Asami away for a romantic weekend, intending to propose, but, after asking him to love her exclusively, she abruptly disappears. Digging into her past, he uncovers disturbing stories of her physical abuse at the hands of her uncle, as well as suggestions she has been involved in murder and abduction. One evening, Asami breaks into Aoyama's house and exacts gruesome revenge for the way she feels Aoyama has betrayed her.

Background

Miike's masterpiece made as much of a splash in the West as *Ring*, its notoriety firmly established when it provoked mass walk-outs during a 2000 Rotterdam Film Festival screening. It put its director firmly on the international map, fuelling interest in his prodigious, uncompromising body of work. *Audition* was based on a novelette by Ryu Murakami, who had directed the art-house S&M flick *Tokyo Decadence* (1991). Aoyama is played by Ryo Ishibashi, who later cropped up in Sono's *Suicide Club* (2001) and the American *The Grudge* (2004) and its sequel, while Miike shrewdly cast a debut actress, ex-Benetton model Eihi Shiina, as the enigmatic Asami.

Verdict

Despite its focus on an unfolding romantic relationship, this is most emphatically *not* a date movie (as some – this writer included – have discovered to their cost). After brilliantly building up a sense of mounting trepidation, Miike unleashes a final-reel assault on his audience's sensibilities that's guaranteed to leave it squirming with fear and disgust. The sight of Asami sheathed in her PVC apron and gauntlets, armed with her acupuncture needles and cheese wire is not something easily dislodged from the subconscious, while her delivery of the phrase 'kiri-kiri-kiri' ('deeper-deeper-deeper') is a horrific masterstroke. Miike delivers one of film history's great story switcheroos, knocking viewers sideways by totally dispensing with the tasteful restraint that has hitherto characterised the film's storytelling. And, as a prelude to his *Grand Guignol* finale, Miike serves up *another* classic shock involving a hideously twitching sack.

As we have seen, Asami is part of a long tradition of wronged and avenging females in Japanese storytelling traditions, and even though she's no ghost there are suggestions that she might be some kind of manifestation of Aoyama's guilt-ridden psyche (he cannot live up to his promise to love only her). The film has been hailed by some feminist critics as a savage critique of the Japanese male view of women (the audition process is demeaning), and definitely reflects a sense that masculinity in modern, post-boom Japan is feeling on the ropes. Nevertheless, Miike makes it impossible to form any pat judgements about his main characters – who both carry painful pasts, and both of whom are guilty of deception – while introducing some intriguing ideas about suffering as a route to personal enlightenment ('To live means to approach death gradually,' Asami sagely informs her lover-victim). Like much of the best Asian horror, *Audition* manages to combine its expertly executed schlock shocks with sociological undercurrents and psychological subtleties, and with this landmark film Miike sends not only our stomachs but also our moral compasses into an unsettling spin.

Uzumaki (2000)

Directed by: Higuchinsky
Cast: Eriko Hatsune (Kirie), Fhi Fan (Shuichi), Hinako Saeki (Kyoko)

Story

High-school student Kirie begins to notice that the population of her hometown, Kurouzu, are becoming obsessed with *uzumaki* (spirals). The father of her boyfriend Shuichi has formed the deepest obsession, keeping a video diary of anything spiral-shaped (including snails). He commits suicide by crawling inside his tumble dryer. The bizarre Uzumaki curse seems to spread: a schoolboy commits suicide by throwing himself down a spiral staircase, a girl starts to sculpt her hair into increasingly elaborate spiral patterns, and another pupil starts to transform into a 'human snail', arriving at school covered in slime. Following her husband's death, Shuichi's mother develops an acute phobia of spirals. With more and more of Kurouzu's population succumbing to the curse, Kirie and Shuichi try to fathom its meaning.

Background

Uzumaki is one of numerous adaptations of the *mangas* of Junji Ito (1963–), worthy of treatment as a Japanese horror *auteur* in his own right. Other notable films based on Ito's work include Norio Tsuruta's *Scarecrow* (2001) about a woman stranded in a village preparing for an annual Scarecrow Festival, and Kazuyuki Shibuya's *Love Ghost* (2001). He is perhaps best known for his series of *Tomie* strips, which have spawned a film franchise with even longer legs than those of *Ring* and *Ju-On*: the current *Tomie* tally of features and V-Cinema films stands at eight. The Tomie character herself is a flirtatious schoolgirl who constantly ends up being murdered by her jealous peers, but supernaturally regenerates, however dismembered her body becomes. The *Uzumaki* film adaptation was helmed by Ukrainian-born Higuchinsky, who had a background in commercials and pop promos and had directed episodes of the *Eko Eko Azarak* TV series, as well as another Ito adaptation, *Long Dream* (2000). He would also direct *TOKYO 10+01* (2003), a film heavily influenced by Fukasaku's *Battle Royale* (2000), in which strangers

– having been fitted with bracelets containing deadly hypodermic needles – are forced to participate in a game to the death.

Verdict

Higuchinsky does an excellent job of bringing Ito's *manga* to life, putting his command of visual effects and digital trickery to impressive use. The episodic nature of the film's plot is actually faithful to the style and presentation of the original strip (as are the sickly green hues that predominate), and the film largely dispenses with conventional plot development in favour of a series of outrageous and impeccably surreal vignettes based on characters succumbing to the 'Uzumaki' spiral shape that gradually sucks the entire town into its vortex. The ensuing physical transformations (a recurring Ito theme) are wildly inventive – from the man coiled in the bottom of his tumble dryer to the humanoid snails crawling up the side of a school. Thankfully, the film doesn't concoct any glib explanations for the phenomenon, allowing events to take on the status of a parable: like Darren Aronofsky's *Pi* (1997), it suggests a concealed, cosmic patterning underpinning our existence which we gradually succumb to and are absorbed into. The overall effect is curiously beautiful as well as deliriously grotesque.

Battle Royale/Batoru Rowaiaru (2000)

Directed by: Kinji Fukasaku
Cast: 'Beat' Takeshi (Kitano), Tatsuya Fujiwara (Shuya), Aki Maeda (Noriko), Taro Yamamoto (Shogo)

'At the dawn of the millennium, the nation collapsed. At fifteen per cent unemployment, ten million were out of work. 800,000 students boycotted school. The adults lost confidence, and fearing the youth, eventually passed the Millennium Educational Reform Act – AKA: The BR Act.'

Prologue to *Battle Royale*

Story

Under the terms of the 'Battle Royale' Act, one class of ninth-grade students is selected annually by lottery, kidnapped, relocated to a deserted island, fitted with electronic explosive collars, given random weapons or tools, and then forced to participate in a three-day survival game in which the last student left alive is the winner. This is the fate that befalls a class of over 40 pupils from Zentsuji Middle School. Kitano, an ex-teacher from the school, gives the class their briefing and then monitors their progress as the death toll steadily rises. Some commit suicide, some form pacts, and some settle old scores. Students who survive the longest include the sweet-natured pair Shuya and Noriko, sadistically vicious Mitsuko, a psychopath called Kazuo who has signed up for his own entertainment, class president Yukie, radical geek Shinji and the enigmatic Shogo, who is seeking to avenge the death of his girlfriend in a previous game.

Background

Based on a popular novel by Koushun Takami, *Battle Royale* became something of a controversial *cause célèbre* on its home turf, spawning a sequel, a *manga* adaptation, numerous fan sites and a mini-industry of memorabilia, whilst prompting calls in the national parliament for its banning on the grounds of the potential harm it might inflict on vulnerable teenagers. Partly as a consequence of this, the film has never secured an official distribution deal in the post-Columbine US (although this may have been because of prohibitive costs as much as squeamishness), while the prospects of a mooted New Line remake have receded since the 2007 Virginia Tech massacre. Despite the film's exploitative premise, veteran director Kinji Fukasaku (1930–2003) claimed to have been inspired by his own first-hand experiences of violence as a teenager during World War Two: his class was conscripted to work in a munitions factory, and during bombing raids people frantically dived under each other to survive; afterwards, he had to help dispose of the blown-up corpses of his friends. Fukasaku's screenwriter son Kenta took over directing duties on the 2003 sequel *Battle Royale II: Requiem* when his father died of prostate cancer after a single day of shooting.

Verdict

While certainly not a traditional horror film, this *sui generis* dystopian fable actually plays as a multi-faceted slasher film, in which grisly deaths are meted out by a range of antagonists in an unpredictable and wholly suspenseful way. The director's seasoned expertise in *yakuza* violence certainly allowed him to orchestrate the various stabbings, shootings, electrocutions and poisonings with considerable panache, creating some chillingly nihilistic characterisations along the way (the mute volunteer psychopath, Kazuo, is utterly dehumanised, while it's easy to appreciate why Quentin Tarantino hired Chiaki Kuriyama to play his schoolgirl assassin in *Kill Bill: Vol 1* (2003) after seeing her as the lethal, switchblade-wielding Takako).

But there are plenty of ideas at play behind the carnage: the film's most blackly comic set-piece – in which a group of girlfriends who have taken refuge in a lighthouse end up killing each other in an escalation of homicidal paranoia – takes a satirical sweep at the ruthless individualism fostered by Japan's ultra-competitive education system. From other angles, the film's intent is more ambivalent. In Takami's novel, the aim of the BR Act is not to stem a rising tide of delinquency but to maintain the power of the totalitarian Japanese empire (which, in this alternative history, survives World War Two) by fostering fear and mistrust. However, the novel's strong anti-authoritarian component is tempered in the film by vivid contemporary fears about the failure of the authorities to deal with rising trends in teenage violence. This ideological ambivalence makes *Battle Royale* a richly fascinating oddity that – in its compelling blend of stylish ultraviolence and sociological engagement – warrants comparison with Kubrick's *A Clockwork Orange* (1971) (a resonance Fukasaku perhaps was aiming for, on the evidence of his pointed classical music cues).

Versus (2000)

Directed by: Ryuhei Kitamura
Cast: Tak Sakaguchi (Prisoner KSC2-303), Hideo Sakaki (Warlock), Chieko Misaka (Girl)

Story

A pair of escaped convicts flee through a forest from some psychotic hitmen, but soon find themselves having to hack their way through hordes of gun-toting *yakuza* zombies bursting out of the forest floor. It transpires that they've stumbled into the Forest of Resurrection, the 444th of the 666 earthly portals to Hell, and a warlock is resurrecting the dead *yakuza* as a prelude to opening the Gate to Hell. One of the convicts turns out to be the resurrected *samurai* warrior who first thwarted the warlock's plans half a millennium ago by robbing him of his blood sacrifice, a beautiful woman. She has now resurrected herself, setting the scene for an epic showdown between the two adversaries.

Background

Director Kitamura (1969–) trained in Australia and delivered an impressive calling card with the low-budget, self-financed *Versus*. He went on to direct the *manga* sci-fi *Alive* (2002), ghost-*samurai* hybrid *Skyhigh* (2003), the ultraviolent *samurai manga* adaptation *Azumi* (2003) and the twenty-eighth Godzilla film, *Godzilla: Final Wars* (2004), which was also the franchise's fiftieth-anniversary film. He recently made his American debut with an adaptation of a Clive Barker *Books of Blood* short story, *The Midnight Meat Train* (2008).

Kitamura owns an independent production company in Tokyo, Napalm Films, and has also directed sequences for the computer game *Metal Gear Solid: The Twin Snakes*.

Verdict

From its opening salvo of lone *samurai* vs zombie carnage, to its left-field, post-apocalyptic coda, Kitamura feeds us a steady stream of what he memorably terms 'Free-Fall Ultra-Violent Non-Stop Entertainment Action'. With its high levels of graphic gore (decapitations, eviscerations, disembowelments) and lashings of jet-black humour (the eyeballs of a *yakuza* zombie end up sticking to his attacker's fingers after he is punched through the head), *Versus* owes obvious debts to other splatter *opuses* like Raimi's *The Evil Dead* and Peter Jackson's *Braindead* (1992), which compensate for low budgets with inventively ostentatious directorial flourishes and gallons of gruesomeness.

If Kitamura's self-consciously cultish film lacks the distinction of those particular classics, it's principally because its overlong narrative seems to be based on the repetitive structure of a 'beat-'em-up' computer game, with the hero confronting a sequential parade of increasingly powerful adversaries. But if the relentless mayhem ultimately proves exhausting, there's still plenty of enjoyment to be had from this film's brazen, pick 'n' mix attitude to genre – ending up as a mongrel hybrid of horror, fantasy, *samurai*, *kung-fu* and *yakuza* flicks – all glued together with a preposterous, era-spanning plot that would make *Highlander* (1986) blush.

Pulse/Kairo (2001)

Directed by: Kiyoshi Kurosawa
Cast: Katou Haruhiko (Ryosuke), Aso Kumiko (Michi), Kenji Mizuhashi (Taguichi), Koyuki (Harue)

Story

Michi, a Tokyo florist, witnesses the suicide of a colleague when she visits his flat to retrieve a computer disc he has been working on. The disc contains images of what seems to be a ghostly otherworld. Student Ryosuke stumbles across a haunted software programme inviting him to 'meet a ghost', and sees disturbing images of figures in rooms. Other characters confront terrifying spectres in 'forbidden rooms', which they then seal off with duct tape. Harue, a supervisor in the computer lab at Ryosuke's university, works out that the spirit realm has finite capacity – meaning that souls are seeping back into the real world via the web. The online users who encounter them become overwhelmed with a sense of their own isolation and loneliness. There is a spate of suicides by young Internet users, and ghostly figures begin appearing in public places before vanishing in a haze of black soot. Society begins to disintegrate, and the streets of Tokyo become a waste ground of smoke and corpses.

Background

The disturbing nature of the *Pulse* experience is partly attributable to writer-director Kiyoshi Kurosawa's conception of ghosts, which is significantly different to the predominant tradition of vengeful *yurei* in Japanese culture. On the R2 Optimum Asia DVD release of the film, he attempts to explain 'a fear that is felt from seeing the lack of something':

> *I've never seen a ghost first hand. But I don't believe that ghosts are full of hatred or resentment or anger. They're commonly portrayed to be filled with emotion, but I think that ghosts are beings that lack human emotion and personality. They're human-like, but all the emotional elements of a normal person are missing: they're empty shells. That's what scares me when it comes to ghosts. In other words, you can just apologise to a ghost that is angry. If that*

ghost is aggressive and attacks you, you can just run away from it. You can try to fight it off or appease it, even if it's useless in the end. But there's no way to appease something that's not there. If a ghost was to appear out of nowhere and you saw it, that's the fear that I think you'd feel.

A poorly received American remake (sample tagline: 'You are now infected') directed by Jim Sonzero and co-written by Wes Craven was released in 2006.

Verdict

Pulse is a film that proves there are strands of modern Japanese horror ambitious enough to engage in head-scratching philosophical speculations while simultaneously delivering some high-quality shudders. Kurosawa shows a blatant disregard for matters of pacing, characterisation and narrative clarity, but his unconventional approach succeeds in creating a film in which the viewer's disorientation gives proceedings the genuine whiff of a waking nightmare. The film has a fair quota of skin-crawling scares (featuring pixillated, jerkily moving wraiths, as well as an unforgettable tower-block suicide jump), but Kurosawa's real achievement is to use low-key techniques to sustain an atmosphere of gnawing unease and pervasive malaise: subtle lighting design (courtesy of Meicho Tomiyama) conjures a world of interior, shadow-drenched gloom and flat, bleak sunlight leeched of warmth. As with the Toronto of Cronenberg's similarly themed *Videodrome* (1983), this is a vision of Tokyo as a city of loneliness and despair, in which all sense of traditional community has vanished. People have become almost wholly isolated from one another, with the nascent technologies of websites and webcams turning us all into virtual presences already almost indistinguishable from ghosts. But despite building to an impressive apocalyptic finale (as his earlier film *Charisma* also did), Kurosawa includes an ocean-set coda that hints at possibilities of renewal.

Dark Water/Honogurai mizu no soko kara (2002)

Directed by: Hideo Nakata
Cast: Hitomi Kuroki (Yoshimi), Rio Kanno (Ikuko), Mirei Oguchi (Mitsuko)

Story

Yoshimi, a young mother in the middle of acrimonious divorce proceedings, moves into a dilapidated apartment block with her five-year-old daughter Ikuko. They are plagued by water dripping through their ceiling from the apartment above, and the apparition of a young girl, Mitsuko, who disappeared from the building a couple of years previously. Ikuko begins to hang out with an 'imaginary friend' while her mother gradually uncovers the disturbing truth about Mitsuko's fate, only gradually comprehending why her spirit is so restless.

Background

Nakata's follow-up to his *Ring* films was also based on a book by Koji Suzuki. Many of the *Ring* production team were rounded up again, including composer Kenji Kawai and cinematographer Junichiro Hayashi. An American remake directed by Walter Salles and starring Jennifer Connelly was released in 2005.

Verdict

From its opening shots of sunlight glancing down through murky water to its emotionally rending climax, Nakata's film is a genuinely class act and one of the true gems of modern J-Horror. The real star of the piece is the dank, decrepit Tokyo apartment block where most of the action is set: it's a fantastically spooky setting, permeated with an air of sadness and loss. As with *Ring*, the narrative's slow-burn pacing and serious-mindedness really help build up a mounting sense of unease, and Nakata's focus on sympathetic, credible characters pays big dividends: Yoshimi is determined to give her young daughter the maternal love she herself was denied as a child, and the viewer can feel her mounting desperation as supernatural events conspire to threaten both her new home and her already-fragile mental state.

Horror fans will find plenty of echoes here of classic western horrors – Mitsuko's shiny mackintosh evokes Nicolas Roeg's *Don't Look Now* (1973), the wall of water cascading from the lift recalls a similar image in Kubrick's *The Shining*, and a moment with a ghostly hand evokes a similarly chilling one in Robert Wise's *The Haunting* (1963). It's a testament to the achievements of Nakata and his collaborators, though, that the film never feels bogged down in self-referentiality, and instead works its own clever and engrossing variations on the classic 'haunted house' genre, fully meriting its own place in the pantheon of all-time great horror movies.

Suicide Circle, aka *Suicide Club/Jisatsu Sakuru* (2002)

Directed by: Shion Sono
Cast: Ryo Ishibashi (Detective Kuroda), Akaji Maro (Detective Murata), Masatoshi Nagase (Detective Shibusawa)

Story

A group of 54 schoolgirls congregate on a platform at Tokyo's Shinjuku Station before jumping in front of a passing train and turning the platform into a bloodbath. Other young people across Japan begin to kill themselves for reasons that remain mysterious. Sports bags are found at the scenes, containing stitched coils of human skin patches. A tip-off from a young hacker calling herself 'The Bat' directs police to a puzzling website that records the suicides with coloured dots before the deaths are even reported. The Bat is then kidnapped by the 'Suicide Club', a radical group headed by a psychopathic weirdo called Genesis. Mitsuko, a girl whose boyfriend has killed himself, discovers that the manufactured, pre-teen, pop-sensation group

'Dessart' have messages urging suicide hidden in secret codes within their lyrics and visuals.

Background

Director Shion Sono (1961–) made a name for himself as an avant-garde poet and underground filmmaker before he hit big with *Suicide Circle*. Following its success, he published a novel (*Suicide Circle: The Complete Edition*) which expanded on the film's story as well as providing material for his tasteful feature follow-up *Suicide Circle 2: Noriko's Dinner Table* (2006). Sono also co-created a *manga* version of *Suicide Circle*, which uses the same mass platform suicide as a kicking-off point but is otherwise very different. Sono has worked across many genres (including, allegedly, gay porn), but horror fans will also want to check out his demented *ero-gro Strange Circus* (2005) and his more conventional J-Horror offering *Exte: Hair Extensions* (2007). *Suicide Circle*'s special effects were masterminded by Yoshihiro Nishimura, who would later direct the gonzo cyberpunk hit *Tokyo Gore Police* (2008).

Verdict

Sono's outrageous film has built itself a strong cult following, and it's easy to see why. Its opening sequence, in which a large group of schoolgirls join hands and chant 'one, two... jump!' before hurling themselves under an oncoming express train and drenching the waiting commuters with gore is unforgettable, and is just the first of several jaw-dropping set-pieces that Sono serves up. One delirious montage intercuts a woman chopping her fingers off while cooking with a girl putting her head in the oven and a street vendor overdosing on pills, while at one point a girl is knocked to the floor by her boyfriend after he has just hurled himself from the roof above. The horror usually arrives laced with jet-black comedy – nowhere more so than when a group of school kids joke that they're going to jump off a roof together, and then half of them actually do.

Police inspector Kuroda (played by Ryo Ishibashi, *Audition*'s hapless widower) is one of the few relatively sane presences in a film largely populated by deviants. Foremost among those is deranged glam rocker Genesis, the self-styled 'Charles Manson of the Information Age', who tortures animals in bags in between singing songs and plotting the destruction of society. Like *Battle Royale*, *Suicide Club* aspires to be a social satire as well as a highly entertaining exploitation pic, but can't seem to make up its mind what its targets are (technological alienation? inane pop music? adolescent fads? existential pretension?) and ends up degenerating into almost total incoherence with its garbled message about the need to connect with yourself. As *Videodrome* showed, though, a film that collapses under the weight of its ideas isn't always a bad thing, and Sono's film leaves the viewer with plenty to ponder as well as a thoroughly churned stomach.

Ju-On: The Grudge (2002)

Directed by: Takashi Shimizu
Cast: Megumi Okina (Rika), Misaki Ito (Hitomi), Misa Uehara (Izumi)

Story

A *Ju-On* is defined as: 'a curse born of a grudge held by someone who dies in the grip of anger. It gathers in the places frequented by that person in life, working itself on those who come into contact with it and thus creating itself anew'.

The film's narrative is divided into six sections, structured in a non-chronological order and spanning several years. Various characters – including new tenants, a social worker and an ex-cop – visit a house in the Tokyo suburbs in which a man, Takeo Saeki, has killed himself along with his wife, Kayako, and young son, Toshio. Gradually, the disparate characters all fall victim to the malevolent spirits haunting the house, which include a black cat and the ghosts of the wife and son.

Background

The director Kiyoshi Kurosawa (*Cure, Pulse*) and *Ring*'s scriptwriter Hiroshi Takahashi are both credited as 'creative consultants' on this J-Horror gem, having mentored director Shimizu at the Tokyo Film Seminar. Like the *Ring* series, the *Ju-On* films have developed into a multimedia, cross-cultural franchise, and Shimizu had already directed two V-Cinema precursors to this feature in 2000, *Ju-On: The Curse* and *Ju-On: The Curse 2*. This film was a reasonable success internationally, paving the way for Shimizu's involvement in the Hollywood remakes.

Verdict

For this writer's money, *Ju-On: The Grudge* is flat out the most frightening of all the modern J-Horrors, fusing the Japanese *kaidan* with modern, US-flavoured techniques to generate multiple indelible moments of sublime, skin-crawling terror. Most of these are masterfully staged by Shimizu using simple physical effects and creative sound design – the creepy ghost-child Toshio opens his mouth and yowls like a cat, while his mother Kayako at one point appears under a victim's bed sheets, crawling up her prone body. The film cannily keeps its audience off balance by fragmenting its story into separate sections and jumbling up the timeframe, depriving us of a conventional protagonist to feel safe with. And neither is there a single 'monster' – as in *The Shining*, the evil forces have a variety of manifestations. But unlike the restless spirits of the Overlook Hotel, these forces are not confined to one locale: although they originate in the haunted suburban Tokyo house at the centre of the narrative, the spooks follow characters to their homes and workplaces (in one shock-cut, Toshio even materialises under a restaurant table). It is possible to detect the influence of the US *Final Destination* series (2000–09), in which a death-force pursues a group of cursed characters, but these hauntings are played with a straight bat rather than an ironic smirk.

Here be monsters: Ishiro Honda's *Godzilla* (1954), Toho Film.

Mask of the demon: Kaneto Shindo's *Onibaba* (1964), Hisao Itoya-Setsuo Noto-Minato.

Tender ministrations: Takashi Miike's *Audition* (1999), Omega Project.

Kept on hold: Takashi Miike's *One Missed Call* (2003), Kadokawa-Daiei Pictures.

A class act: Kinji Fukasaku's *Battle Royale* (2000), Battle Royale Production Committee.

Twisted thoughts: Higuchinsky's *Uzumaki* (2000), Omega Micott.

Posters for Kiyoshi Kurosawa's *Pulse* (2001, Daiei/Hakuhodo/Imagica/NTV), Hideo Nakata's *Kaidan* (2007, Avex Entertainment), Takashi Shimizu's *Ju-On: The Grudge* (2002, Aozora, Nikkatsu/OZ Company) and Chan-wook Park's *Thirst* (2009, CJ Entertainment/ Focus Features/Universal Pictures).

Posters for Chan-wook Park's *Old Boy* (2003, Egg Films/Show East), Hideo Nakata's *L: Change the World* (2007, L Film Partners/Nikkatsu), Ji-woon Kim's *A Tale of Two Sisters* (2003, BOM Films/Masulpiri Films) and Shinya Tsukamoto's *Tetsuo II: Body Hammer* (1992, Kaijyu Theatre Co/ Toshiba EMI).

Body horror: Kiyoshi Kurosawa's *Retribution* (2006), OZ Company.

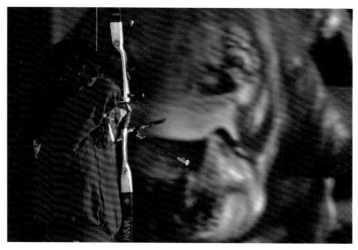

Shoot to kill: Joon-ho Bong's *The Host* (2006), Chungeorahm Film/Showbox Entertainment.

Only the freshest ingredients: Fruit Chan's *Dumplings* (2004), Applause Pictures.

Seeing red: Banjong and Parkpoom's *Shutter* (2004), GMM/Phenomena.

Poison pen letters: Kaneko Shusuke's *Death Note* (2006), Death Note Film Partners/ Nikkatsu.

Out on a limb: Shinya Tsukamoto's *Haze* (2005), Gold View Co.

There are social subtexts for those on the lookout: the neglected elderly woman discovered in the house by the social worker is symptomatic of the breakdown in traditional Shinto values and obligations, as is the perceived infidelity that acted as the catalyst for the original murders. But there's no doubt that Shimizu's primary aim here is to scare our socks off, which he does with considerable panache. It's a shame that the film and its remakes have been branded as 'The Grudge' rather than the more appropriate 'The Curse' (used for the earlier video films), as it is the motiveless malevolence of the film's supernatural forces that helps make this film such an effective shocker.

Marebito, aka *The Stranger From Afar* (2004)

Directed by: Takashi Shimizu
Cast: Shinya Tsukamoto (Masuoka), Tomomi Miyashita ('F'), Kazuhiro Nakahara (Arei Furoki)

Story

Freelance cameraman Masuoka is determined to fathom the nature of true fear. He obsesses over footage he has captured of a subway suicide, in which a man stabs himself through the eye while facing an unseen antagonist. Returning to the suicide scene, Masuoka discovers a doorway to a subterranean civilisation. Here he encounters the spirit of the suicide victim and a naked, chained, mute girl, whom he christens 'F'. He brings her home, where he discovers that she needs to feed on blood to survive. A woman confronts him about the whereabouts of his daughter, Fuyumi. What follows is an escalation of madness and murder, culminating in Masuoka achieving a more perfect appreciation of terror's face.

Background

In 2004, the Film School of Tokyo collaborated with the city's Eurospace Cinema exhibition/distribution outfit on an experimental

'*Bancho*' project. This scheme – inspired by the Danish *Dogme* model – aimed to produce a series of innovative, low-budget horror, comedy and *pinku* films directed by a mixture of film students and established pros. The horror entries were supervised by Hiroshi Takahashi, the screenwriter of the early *Ring* and *Ju-On* films, who made his directing debut with the tongue-in-cheek horror *Town of Sodom* (2004). Shimizu seems to have embraced the opportunity to return to his roots in V-Cinema (his original *Ju-On* films were made for Toei Video), and he shot *Marebito* in just eight days on digital tape. Its rough-hewn, DIY aesthetic was clearly influenced by the early work of Shinya Tsukamoto who – in a clear gesture of homage – Shimizu cast as his obsessive protagonist Masuoka.

Verdict

It's easy to see why Shimizu – having tethered himself so firmly to the seemingly unending *Ju-On* franchise – seized on the opportunity to tackle some different material, especially something as conceptually rich as *Marebito*. His *Ju-On* films certainly made audiences jump, but this film is a genuine attempt to get under the skin in a more profound way. The result is a heady brew of disturbing images and enigmatic ideas that – if finally a little too opaque and pretentious for its own good – is still one of the most original and unsettling of modern Japanese horror films.

Screenwriter-novelist Chiaki Konaka stirs plenty into the mix: he name-checks the 'Hollow Earth' theories developed by Theosophical Society founder Madame Blavatsky, as well as the pulp sci-fi novelist Richard Shaver (a regular in *Amazing Stories* magazine), who claimed to be stalked by demonic entities he called 'Deros' (a contraction of 'detrimental robots'). The filmic representation of these creatures is influenced by the work of *manga* artist Morohoshi. There are also references to HP Lovecraft's Mountains of Madness, the legend of the feral foundling Kaspar Hauser and the urban legends that have persisted since the Edo era about a subterranean world concealed beneath Tokyo.

All these ideas contribute to the film's conceit about terror being a form of ancient wisdom, sealed in the subconscious mind but an inextricable part of the human condition. Thankfully, these ideas add layers of intrigue to the narrative rather than overwhelming it, and the film's more fantastic elements most probably represent the psychic dislocation of its troubled protagonist – who is perhaps wrestling with the real-world issues of urban alienation, technological overload and acute familial dysfunction rather than literal demons and devils.

Rampo Noir/Rampo Jigoku (2005)

Directed by: Suguru Takeuchi, Akio Jissoji, Hisayasu Sato, Atsushi Kaneko
Cast: Tadanobu Asano (Various Roles), Ryuhei Matsuda, Mikako Ichikawa

Story

This film is an anthology of four adaptations of Edogawa Rampo stories. In *Mars's Canal*, a man, having murdered his lover, stumbles naked across a barren landscape towards a lake. In *Mirror Hell*, Detective Akechi (Asano) investigates a series of deaths at a traditional teahouse, in which women have been discovered with their faces melted off. He traces the murders to a local mirror-maker obsessed with the medieval legend of a lethal 'shadow mirror'. *Caterpillar* explores the sado-masochistic erotic bond between a limbless war veteran and his wife. *Crawling Bugs* involves a man who develops a jealous obsession with the theatre star that he chauffeurs around, which then degenerates into insanity and perversion.

Background

Edogawa Rampo had always been a significant influence on Japanese horror cinema, with filmmakers finding rich pickings in his highly visual style of storytelling and penchant for exploring relationships between men and women that were simultaneously highly destructive and perversely passionate. His style of *ero-gro* (blending mystery, violence and erotica) inspired superior *pinkus* like *Blind Beast* and *Horrors of Malformed Men*, and recent years have seen the biographical *Rampo* (1994) – released to mark the centenary of the author's birth – Tsukamoto's *Gemini* (1999) and this anthology piece. *Rampo Noir* brought together two cult auteurs – Hisayasu Sato (*Splatter: Naked Blood*) and Akio Jissoji (a prolific director whose output spanned children's TV shows and Nikkatsu *pinkus*) – with *manga* artist Atsushi Kaneko and commercials and promo whiz Suguru Takeuchi.

Verdict

While not quite as successful in its execution as might have been hoped, this ambitious project contains enough stylistic invention and disturbing imagery to stand as a prime example of the continuing artistic health of the Asian horror sector. In a market somewhat oversaturated with vengeful spooks and J-Horror clichés, its emphasis on psychological terrors over supernatural scares is particularly refreshing. Takeuchi's wordless opening salvo, *Mars's Canal*, half buries its images of violence and debasement under a flurry of scratchy edits and sonic crescendos, its abstraction clearly signalling that these adaptations will push the envelope. Jissoji's instalment, *Mirror Hell*, is the most conventional in its presentation, showcasing the sleuthing of Japan's most famous literary gumshoe, Detective Akechi, as he works up a rational solution to seemingly supernatural killings. Elegantly shot and designed, it still finds space for an S&M digression involving lashings of hot wax, as well as the memorable spectacle of the narcissistic artisan at the centre of the investigation sealing himself inside a sphere with a completely mirrored interior in pursuit of cosmic revelation. As *Blind Beast* earlier demonstrated, Rampo's work is often concerned with explorations of extreme aesthetics, and Sato's *Caterpillar* depicts a wife using radical surgery to turn her husband into a work of living art: desperate for him not to return to a war that has already deformed him, she shapes his stricken torso into her 'caterpillar' as a simultaneous gesture of love and disgust. As his *manga* background might have led us to expect, Kaneko's final segment, *Crawling Bugs*, serves up a visual feast, incorporating highly stylised, colour-saturated sets and *noir*-ish costumes to add an ironic sheen of romanticism to its tale of necrophilic madness. All four sections of *Rampo Noir* feature cult star Tadanobu Asano, who appeared in Oshima's *Gohatto* (1999) and Kitano's *Zatoichi* (2003), as well as Kiyoshi Kurosawa's *Bright Future* (2003).

Death Note/Desu Noyo (2006)

Directed by: Kaneko Shusuke
Cast: Tatsuya Fujiwara (Light), Ken'ichi Matsuyama ('L'), Erika Toda (Misa), Asaka Seto (Naomi)

Story

Law student Light Yagami discovers a mysterious notebook entitled 'Death Note'. The instructions inside state that if a person's name is written down in it they will die; in addition, the cause of death can be specified. Light experiments with the names of criminals, and discovers that the book is as good as its word. Desiring a crime-free world, he becomes fêted as a moral serial killer (dubbed 'Kira') and a cult hero to many members of the public. He is visited by Ryuk, an apple-eating *shinigami* ('god of death') visible only to him, and who starts to act as his confidant. Light continues to kill anyone he believes deserves to die. Light's father Yagami, a police chief, is placed in charge of an international investigation into the killings. He communicates with a mysterious detective known only as 'L'. Light uses Raye, an FBI agent, to get the names of his colleagues, who he then kills. 'L' reveals himself to Yagami's team – he is a young student of about Light's age. The stage is set for a battle of wills between the two devious adversaries.

Background

Director Shusuke (who made the *Gamera* trilogy of *kaiju eiga* in the nineties) shot this film virtually back-to-back with its sequel *Death Note: The Last Name* (2006), which was released in Japan only five months after the original: the two are clearly conceived as one piece, with the first film setting up the context for the complex cat-and-mouse game that develops between the 'moral' serial killer, Light, and the introverted misfit, 'L'. Both were adapted from a *manga* written by Tsugumi Ohba and illustrated by Takeshi Obata. Produced by Nippon Television and shot on HD rather than film, both films made sizeable splashes at the Japanese box office, paving the way for a further spin-off *L: Change the World* (2008), directed by Hideo Nakata. A Hollywood remake of Shusuke's film is in the pipeline.

Verdict

This entertaining blend of horror flick, serial-killer thriller and teen melodrama shows that – in an era of diminishing returns from *yurei* – Japanese horror still has a few fresh ideas up its sleeve. The story cleverly taps into concerns about the ease with which bullies can indulge in character assassination on Internet blogs, message boards and chatrooms – no doubt partly accounting for the popularity of the *manga* and film(s) with young audiences. The film's teen-appeal is further boosted by the casting of charismatic stars Tatsuya Fujiwara (Shuya in *Battle Royale*) and Ken'ichi Matsuyama. With its emphasis on psychological games rather than kinetic action, the film is visually fairly conservative, with the honourable exception of the *shinigami* Ryuk – a hulking CGI ghoul with bat wings and filed teeth, decked out in Gothic accessories and munching on red apples (emblems of temptation?). This particular devil certainly exists in the details, and it is *Death Note*'s eccentric touches – L's insatiable sugar craving, a TV screen crucially hidden in a bag of crisps, the sheer strangeness of its very premise – that make it such an intriguing oddity.

TAKA ICHISE AND J-HORROR THEATRE

One of the major movers-and-shakers on the modern Japanese film scene, Ichise had a hand in many landmark Asian horrors. Before producing Nakata's *Ring* he notched up several major successes made through his own production company Oz Co and the LA-based indie OZLA Pictures, which he set up in 1992. These included the 1993 action thriller *American Yakuza* (starring Viggo Mortensen) and the Russell Crowe vehicle *No Way Back* (1995), as well as Christopher Gans' hit *Crying Freeman* (1996). After the success of *Ring* and its partner film *Spiral*, Ichise went on to produce – among many others – *Ring 2*, *Ring 0: Birthday*, *Dark Water*, *Ju-On: The Grudge* and *Ju-On: The Grudge 2* (as well as their video precursors and Hollywood remakes), before launching the J-Horror Theatre series.

This ambitious project has become something of a series manqué. Originally, Ichise had rounded up six directors to each make a horror feature to be released under the J-Horror Theatre banner for Toho. The line-up consisted of Hideo Nakata, Kiyoshi Kurosawa, Takashi Shimizu, Norio Tsuruta, Masayuki Ochiai, and *Ring* scriptwriter Hiroshi Takahashi. To date, the series appears to have either stalled or mutated from its original concept, with only three of the proposed six films having been released under the banner; Kurosawa's *Retribution* and Nakata's *Kaidan* were released separately, while Takahashi's film has yet to materialise.

However, the quality of the offerings served up as the J-Horror Theatre brand was sufficiently high to make its apparent demise regrettable. Ochiai's *Infection* (2004) was first out of the gate, and was based on an episode of the TV series *Tales of the Unusual*, first broadcast in Japan in 1991 and also directed by Ochiai. Set over a single night in an understaffed hospital where a fatal medical blunder is being covered up, the film builds up an impressively clammy sense of claustrophobia as the titular virus spreads through the patients and staff, reducing many to liquefied green goo. It gradually emerges that the infection is a kind of mental derangement affecting the subconscious mind, and that various overlapping realities are at play in the mind of lead doctor Dr Akiba. As well as serving up some slick narrative switches, Ochiai misses no opportunity to use his medical paraphernalia to make us squirm: notable instances include a nurse placing her hands in the scalding water of a sterilisation tank and another practicing needle injections on herself. Dispensing regular doses of black humour ('Nurse Shiozaki's internal organs are gone!') and refreshingly devoid of traditional ghosts and ghouls, the film was a commendable attempt to broaden the scope of J-Horror's palette.

The same was true of Tsuruta's *Premonition* (2004), based on the 1973 *manga Newspaper of Terror* by Jiro Tsunoda; it plays as a variant on the likes of *The Dead Zone* (1983) and *The Butterfly Effect* (2004), in which psychic windows onto the future raise vexed questions of personal responsibility and the nature of destiny. While uploading a file for work via a payphone, high-school teacher Hideki (Hiroshi Makami) discovers a page from a newspaper foretelling the death of his five-year-old daughter in a freak road accident: paralysed with confusion, he fails to prevent the horrific events playing out before his eyes. Three years on, he starts receiving further premonitions of gruesome deaths, while his estranged wife conducts her own investigations into paranormal activity and the phenomenon of prophetic newspapers. After teaming up to investigate the fates of others with similar clairvoyant abilities, Hideki realises that it is within his power to alter events – even those from the past – but at a tremendous physical cost to himself. As with *Infection*, this conceit allows for some disorientating shifts between different parallel realities – only here the drama remains rooted in the moving dynamics of a damaged family struggling to heal itself. More sombre and restrained than Ochiai's entry in the series, Tsuruta keeps the shock quotient low in favour of a cumulative emotional charge.

The remaining 'official' J-Horror Theatre entry was Shimizu's *Reincarnation* (2005), which revisited some of the themes of his *Ju-On* films, but on a larger canvas. Nagisa is an actress hired to star in a horror film set in a Tokyo hotel that recreates a massacre carried out 20 years before by a deranged professor. Cast as the killer's murdered daughter, Nagisa finds herself haunted by visions of the actual events – intensified by the fact that they are currently filming at the original site of the crimes. She discovers an 8mm film camera that could contain footage of the murders, while a creepy doll that belonged to one of the victims starts to take on a vengeful life of its own. Shot on a relatively large budget of $4 million, *Reincarnation* possesses the visual slickness and ambitious production design that you would expect from a director with Hollywood experience under his belt. With its focus on evil forces adhering to a specific site where a man has murdered his family, the film links back to the *Ju-On* series, and through it to *The Shining* – a major touchstone for much J-Horror, and this film in particular (with its cavernous abandoned hotel). Like Kubrick, Shimizu gets decent mileage out of playing with the concept of 'cryptomnesia' (memory bias), with supernatural visions, memories and the simulacra of filmic fictions all mingling in Nagisa's mind during the final act to intriguing effect. Shimizu also confirms his mastery of scare tactics: the mechanical doll who insists that she and the protagonist remain 'Together Forever' is memorably unnerving. But unfortunately for the J-Horror Theatre brand, the film's sophistication didn't translate into domestic box office, leaving Ichise's ambitious project in limbo for the time being.

KOREAN HORROR CINEMA

RUPTURES AND SCHISMS

Since the massive success of Je-gyu Kang's breakthrough action blockbuster *Shiri* (1999), Korean cinema has been enjoying something of a golden age, reflected in a steady stream of high-profile international successes from *Joint Security Area* (2000) and *Old Boy* (2003) to *The Host* (2006) and *The Good, the Bad and the Weird* (2008). These films have been whipping up plenty of enthusiasm on home turf: by 2005, South Korea actually held the distinction of watching more domestic films than foreign imports.

Korean cinema may be a genuine twenty-first-century success story, but its time in the limelight has only finally materialised after decades of colonial control, civil war and state repression. In the 1910–45 period, Korea was occupied by the Japanese, and the country's films were used almost exclusively as propaganda tools for the colonial regime. In 1938, the Japanese took over all of the country's filmmaking, and by 1942 the use of the Korean language in films was banned outright. Following the defeat of the Japanese in World War Two, Korea was divided into two ideologically distinct zones, laying the groundwork for the South's invasion by the Communist North in 1950 and the subsequent devastation of the three-year Korean War (during which much of Korea's early cinematic record was incidentally destroyed). North Korea, of course, has remained one of the world's most secretive states ever since, and – by all accounts – its film industry is dominated by crude propagandistic fables that toe the socialist-realist party line.

For South Korea, the first green shoots of their post-war cinematic flowering appeared in the mid-fifties, when tax breaks seeded a fresh wave of films. Several psychological horror films emerged during this era, centred around claustrophobic domestic spaces – Ki-yeong Kim's *The Housemaid* (1960) is a strong example. Throughout the sixties and seventies, there was a vogue for ghost stories (*kuei-dam*) featuring vengeful spirits that ran parallel to the Japanese *kaidan eiga* boom. As might be expected, South Korea maintained a complex, uneasy relationship with its former coloniser (which remains to this day), trying to maintain an independent identity while inevitably feeling the pull of its cultural gravitational field (1999's *The Ring Virus* was a Korean remake of Nakata's hit that tried to trump it in fidelity to Suzuki's novel); Korea even produced its own versions of *kaiju eiga* like *Yonggary, Monster from the Deep* (1967).

In the seventies, however, the industry fell into decline as social turmoil overtook South Korea in the shape of a military *coup d'état*, a presidential assassination and bloody public suppressions by the army. Films once again became co-opted as propaganda tools as the new dictatorship tried to tighten its grip. The following decade saw a gradual transition towards democracy and a relinquishing of protectionism. In 1988, foreign films were allowed access to the Korean marketplace, putting pressure on the domestic industry to raise its game. When the military dictatorship (and its attendant censorship) ended in 1992, the conditions were ripe for a creative and commercial resurgence. The introduction of film schools, the entrepreneurialism of private investors (who filled a vacuum after the late-nineties Asian financial crisis curbed the involvement of big corporations) and the financial input of the Film Promotion Corporation encouraged a new climate of risk-taking and aesthetic ambition. The Pusan Film Festival – close to Seoul – soon became dubbed the 'Sundance of the East'.

With a century of repression behind them, it's hardly surprising that many of South Korea's new-wave filmmakers have tackled stories and themes that reflect their nation's turbulent past. The desire for reunification with the estranged North is explicit in Chan-wook Park's *Joint Security Area*, but exists as a strong subtext in films like *The Isle* (2000), horror-war hybrid *R-Point* (2004) and *The Host*. The conflicts and divisions that afflict the family unit in many horror films (*A Tale of Two Sisters* [2003], *Phone*, *Acacia* [2003], *The Host*) – seem to reflect the wider ruptures in the nation's fabric (as well as unease about the effects of rapid modernisation on a traditionally very conservative culture). Film critic Jamie Russell has pointed out that the Korean concept of 'Han' – a feeling of deep sadness that clings to unhealed psychological wounds, particularly those connected to the national schism – is writ large in works like *The Isle*, and by extension the films of Chan-wook Park's 'Vengeance Trilogy'.

As would also be expected in a fledgling democracy, a strong streak of anti-authoritarianism connects much of the new cinema. *Whispering Corridors* (1998) – positioned at the vanguard of the new 'K-Horror' wave that has paralleled the J-Horror boom – is a fierce indictment of the strict conformity of South Korea's education system, a microcosm of the larger society, while *The Host* is scathing of the way the Korean authorities collude with the American military at the expense of the blue-collar Seoul folk they are supposed to protect.

To an even greater extent than its Japanese counterpart, the new wave of Korean horror is characterised by an elastic approach to genre. Tales of vengeful ghosts have continued to feature – Tae-gyung Kim's *The Ghost* (2004) was a slick if derivative recent addition – but there has been a clear ambition on the part of some Korean filmmakers to stake out fresh territory. This has been most evident in the wilfully hard-to-categorise work of Chan-wook Park and Ki-duk Kim, but equally applies to Ji-woon Kim's jet-black comedy-horror *The Quiet Family* (1998), the dementedly grotesque psychological horror of Jun-hwen Jeong's *Save the Green Planet* (2003), Sung-ho

Kim's *Into the Mirror* (2003) – a cop thriller set largely in a haunted department store in which characters' reflections take on a lethal life of their own – and the aforementioned *R-Point* (2004), about a spectral combat unit during the Vietnam War. The recent release of Pil-sung Yim's dark fantasy chiller *Hansel & Gretel* (2007) proves that fusing different traditions of cinematic storytelling has become something of a Korean specialty. This flexible attitude to genre has been aided and abetted by the impressive versatility of some of Korea's charismatic new breed of stars – like Kang-ho Song, Min-sik Choi and Ha-kyun Shin – who are clearly game for just about any challenge that's thrown at them.

A CURIOUS CASE: SANG-OK SHIN

Shin was a prolific Korean filmmaker who had made several creditable *kuei-dam*, including *The Snake Woman* (1969), in which a Buddhist monk is seduced by the titular demon who wants him to sire her unholy offspring, *Ghosts of Chosun* (1970), in which a lecherous nobleman receives his comeuppance courtesy of a pair of spooks he harried to the grave, and the intriguingly titled *Woman With Half a Soul* (1973). In a bizarre turn of events, Shin and his wife were, by their own account, kidnapped by North Korean agents in the late-seventies and whisked off to Pyongyang, where he was tasked by the film-loving dictator Jong-il Kim with reviving the film industry. His assignment was *Pulgasari* (1985), a remake of an earlier monster movie about an iron-eating lizard who defends the peasantry against oppression, which was intended to play as a kind of 'communist Godzilla'. Shin escaped in 1986 when Kim allowed him to travel to Vienna to make a distribution deal for the movie.

KOREAN MODERN HORROR MASTERS

KI-HYUNG PARK

Park's early short *Great Pretenders* (1996) scooped up several international awards, paving the way for his landmark debut feature *Whispering Corridors* (1998), which ushered in a new wave of supernatural Korean horror films that would soon be dubbed 'K-Horror'. The film's blend of ghostly mystery with high-school soap operatics proved influential, spawning a mini subgenre of loose sequels and imitators. Park followed up with paranormal romance *Secret Tears* (2000), before delivering the fascinating horror oddity *Acacia* (2003). It is regrettable that Park is not more prolific – in recent years his only offering has been the violent high-school-gang thriller *Gangster High* (2006).

Key Horror Works

Whispering Corridors (1988), *Acacia* (2003)

JI-WOON KIM

Like other Korean directors, Kim (1964–) has a body of work that demonstrates a mastery of multiple genres: his most recent film is the spaghetti-Western spoof *The Good, the Bad and the Weird* (2008). He cut his teeth directing plays before making his film debut with *The Quiet Family* (1998), starring future Korean superstars Min-sik Choi and Kang-ho Song. This impressive horror-comedy about a dysfunctional family running a remote mountain lodge whose guests keep dying was later refashioned by Takashi Miike into his deranged zombie-musical *The Happiness of the Katakuris* (2001). Kim's next horror offering was *Memories* – a segment of Applause's pan-Asian anthology *Three* (2002), which also featured contributions from Nimibutr Nonzee and Peter Chan. The story of a man slowly realising that he has chopped up his wife when she was on the point of leaving him, *Memories* was a dry run for themes of psychological trauma and character fissioning that would find spectacular expression in Kim's next feature, the brilliant *A Tale of Two Sisters* (2003). Kim's non-horror films, *The Foul King* (2000) – about a bank clerk who turns into a professional masked wrestler – and the violent gangster thriller *A Bittersweet Life* (2005), have also met with acclaim.

Key Horror Works

The Quiet Family (1998), *Memories* (segment of *Three*, 2002), *A Tale of Two Sisters* (2003)

BYUNG-KI AHN

Director Ahn (1967–) has built up a solid track record in the horror genre since his serviceable debut, the college-set vengeful spook thriller *Nightmare* (2000) – aka *Horror Game Movie*. His sophomore effort *Phone* (2002) reunited him with the actress Ji-won Ha, and was a prime slice of K-Horror that demonstrated Ahn's considerable technical mastery. He followed up with *Bunshinsaba* (2004) in which a high-school girl becomes possessed (after a Ouija board session) by the vengeful spirit of a dead classmate persecuted by school bullies. Ahn's most recent offering has been the 'webcomic' adaptation *APT* (2006), in which a woman moves into a high rise and notices that a spate of deaths in the apartments opposite coincides with the lights all simultaneously turning off. While much of Ahn's output is derivative and lacking in the stamp of originality that marks Korea's best auteurs, his work is consistently entertaining and demonstrates that, in the field of slick scares, he is rarely less than an accomplished genre craftsman.

Key Horror Works

Nightmare (2000), *Phone* (2002), *Bunshinsaba* (2004), *APT* (2006)

CHAN-WOOK PARK

Park (1963–) grew up in Seoul and studied philosophy at Sogang University, where he founded a film club and published articles on cinema; it was seeing Hitchcock's *Vertigo* (1958) that apparently fired his ambition to become a filmmaker. After working briefly as an assistant director, he made his debut with the romantic thriller *The Moon is… the Sun's Dream* in 1992. Throughout the nineties, he was better known as a film critic than as a director – a state of affairs that changed radically with the release of *Joint Security Area* (2000) – a military thriller dramatising the cold-war tensions that still define relations between North and South Korea – which proved a massive commercial and critical smash. This success afforded him enough creative freedom to embark on the steely, shocking *Sympathy for Mr Vengeance* (2002), a contemporary horror-tragedy rooted in Senecan and Jacobean traditions of bloody vengeance. The film balances its 'sympathies' between a deaf-mute factory worker who kidnaps the daughter of a wealthy industrialist to finance his sister's kidney transplant and the vengeful businessman who tracks down his daughter's abductor after the blackmail transaction tragically backfires. The uncomfortable questions raised by the film about the justifications for violence and the corrosive effects suffering can have on an individual's moral bearings were revisited in Park's *Old Boy* (2003), an equally bravura piece of modern filmmaking that deservedly became an international cult hit. Two years later, he returned with *Lady Vengeance* (2005), the third part of what subsequently became known as his 'Vengeance Trilogy', climaxing with the blood-curdling revenge a woman takes after a long incarceration on the monstrous child-killer who framed her for murder. While not marketed as horror films, these works explored psychological anguish and extreme mental states, and were steeped in enough incidences of squirm-inducing graphic violence to feel *overwhelmingly* horrific.

In between these projects, he contributed *Cut* to the 2004 pan-Asian anthology *Three... Extremes* (a follow-up to the original *Three*), a baroque chamber-piece in which an embittered film extra plays sadistic mind games with a complacent director: he presents him with the choice of either strangling a kidnapped child or watching helplessly as he chops off the fingers of his trussed-up pianist wife. Some commentators have plausibly suggested that the piece is a coded expression of Park's personal guilt at his own meteoric professional success. After the maudlin, CGI-drenched diversion of *I'm a Cyborg, But That's OK* (2006), Park returned to horror territory with *Thirst* (2009) – starring the ubiquitous Kang-ho Song – concerning a priest who becomes a vampire after a botched medical experiment.

Key Horror Works

Sympathy for Mr Vengeance (2002), *Old Boy* (2003), *Cut* (2004), *Lady Vengeance* (2005), *Thirst* (2009)

MODERN KOREAN HORROR: ESSENTIAL VIEWING

Whispering Corridors/Yeogo Goedam (1998)

Directed by: Ki-hyung Park
Cast: Mi-yun Lee (Eun-yung), Gyu-ri Kim (Ji-oh), Kang-hie Choi (Jae-yi)

Story

At a private, all-girls high school, teacher Mrs Park is found hanged one morning. Just before her death, she has made a discovery about Jin-ju, a girl who committed suicide in the school's art room several years before. The headmaster makes the pupils swear not to spread rumours about Mrs Park's death. Ex-pupil Eun-yung, who had once been prevented by Mrs Park from befriending Jin-ju, returns to the school as a replacement tutor. Schoolgirl Ji-oh, who seems to be able to commune with the dead, paints a disturbing image of Mrs Park's face. The headmaster, having made sexual advances towards one of the girls, is violently killed by supernatural forces. As the body count rises further, Eun-yung and Ji-oh realise that Jin-ju's unquiet spirit is seeking revenge on those who rejected her and are perpetuating the school's culture of loneliness.

Background

One of the films that kicked off the late-nineties South East Asian horror boom, *Whispering Corridors* was a domestic hit and spawned several unofficial 'sequels' set in similar environments but featuring no continuity of plot or character: 1999's impressive *Memento Mori*, whose central lesbian relationship ruffled the feathers of South Korea's conservative establishment; 2003's *Wishing Stairs*, which mixes its story of backstage rivalry at a ballet school with a legend about a fox spirit who grants wishes when invoked on the twenty-ninth step of a staircase; 2005's *Voice*, featuring the ghost of a murdered singer who teams up with a friend to unravel the reasons for her death; and 2009's *A Blood Pledge*, whose title refers to a suicide pact at a Catholic girls' school.

Verdict

Taking its place in an honourable tradition of genre films and TV series encompassing *Suspiria*, *Carrie* (1976), *Buffy the Vampire Slayer*, the Japanese *Haunted School* TV series and *Eko Eko Azarak: Wizard of Darkness* (1995), Park's debut feature proves once again that pedagogical institutions are unparalleled hotbeds of horror. And these eponymous corridors are particularly rife with fear and loathing, thanks to a head teacher who insists on his pupils treating each other as competitors and enemies rather than allies. The Korean education system has a reputation for toughness, and it's easy to see why this film's overt attacks on bullying authoritarianism and meek conformism would have struck a big chord on native soil.

Park's film benefits from some finely honed characterisations, and this particular subgenre of Korean high-school horror focuses as much on building up complex, psychologically plausible relationships between its troubled teenagers as it does on delivering the requisite scares. There are a small number of gory set-pieces, but elsewhere the supernatural scenes are staged with beguiling simplicity – a spectre is propelled down a corridor in a succession of rapid jump cuts, panes of glass blowing out on either side, while the shots of blood running down classroom walls or seeping from a statuette of lonely Jin-ju are truly haunting.

The Isle/Seom (2000)

Directed by: Ki-duk Kim
Cast: Jung Seo (Hee-jin), Yu-suk Kim (Hyun-shik), Sung-hee Park (Eun-a)

Story

Hee-jin is a girl in charge of renting out a group of fishing huts on a remote mountain lake to male visitors. She provides them with all their supplies, as well as arranging for local prostitutes to visit. Occasionally, she performs sexual services herself for extra money. Hyun-shik, a former policeman on the run after perpetrating a crime of passion, checks into one of the huts and prepares to commit suicide, but Hee-jin intervenes to stop him. The seeds of romance are sown, but he quickly oversteps the mark by attempting to rape her. The police arrive and Hyun-shik panics and unsuccessfully attempts suicide by swallowing a line of fish hooks and then yanking the wire. Hee-jin helps him hide in the water beneath the hut, and makes love to him after hauling him out. Hee-jin grows jealous of Hyun-shik's friendship with a local prostitute, leading to her accidental death. When the dead girl's violent pimp arrives, Hee-jin and Hyun-shik drown him. Terrified that Hyun-shik will leave her, Hee-jin mutilates her vagina with a line of fish hooks. The bodies of the prostitute and her pimp are discovered, forcing the lovers to flee.

Background

Ki-duk Kim (1960–) has proved a highly mercurial talent, escaping easy pigeon-holing by creating a body of work that – while fixated on social outcasts of various types – is massively idiosyncratic and largely *sui generis*. Several of his films – including his debut *Crocodile* (1996), *The Isle*, *Bad Guy* (2001), *Samaritan Girl* (2004) and *The Bow* (2005) – are concerned with symbiotic sado-masochistic relationships between men and women, and feature bursts of graphically intense violence. But his filmography features an equal smattering of gentler and more restrained films like *The Birdcage Inn* (1998), the Buddhist fable *Spring, Summer, Autumn, Winter... and Spring* (2003) and *3-Iron* (2004).

Many of Kim's films are pictorially striking, perhaps reflecting the years he spent training as a painter in Paris in the early nineties before discovering his cinematic vocation. He also had stints as a marine, a seminary student and a factory worker. Kim apparently had a fractious, abusive relationship with his father, a disabled veteran, which fuelled some of his explorations of violence in films like *The Isle*. His fifth feature, and made on a low budget with no star names, it fared badly at the domestic box office but became his international breakthrough after gaining notoriety on the festival circuit for its scenes involving fish-hook mutilations and conspicuous cruelty towards fish and frogs (a Venice screening allegedly prompted walk-outs and faintings).

Verdict

The Isle offers proof positive that 'Asian horror' contains more diversity within its porous borders than is sometimes assumed, and this bizarrely beautiful – if occasionally gruelling – slice of psychological horror is a welcome tonic after hordes of vengeful spooks and technological terrors. The film's notoriously extreme imagery of bodily mutilation and animal mistreatment is certainly hard to stomach, and there is a lingering suspicion that the latter, like the atrocities perpetrated against actual animals in Italian *mondo* cannibal films of the seventies and eighties – are included to intensify the sense of (faked) violence against humans. Nevertheless, the nature of violence repeatedly surfaces as a key theme in Kim's work, and is not something he trivialises: his characters are verbally inarticulate, frequently communicating their emotional needs through inflicting excruciating pain on themselves and others (occasionally with the aforementioned fish hooks). The film's sparse dialogue, lyrical, piano-based score and haunting, mist-drenched, mountain-lake setting combine beautifully for this tale of two lonely souls clumsily fumbling their way through a series of melancholy miscommunications towards a fragile, hard-won happiness. Although it builds to a startlingly surreal final image that suggests redemptive possibilities, *The Isle* remains a stark, unflinching exploration of the sado-masochistic core that many love affairs are built around, and is a study in psychological perversity to rank alongside Masumura's *Blind Beast* and Miike's *Audition*.

Phone/Pon (2002)

Directed by: Byung-ki Ahn
Cast: Ji-won Ha (Ji-won), Yu-mi Kim (Ho-jung), Seo-woo Eun (Yung-ju)

Story

Having uncovered a sex scandal, Seoul journalist Ji-won lies low in a house owned by Chang-hoon, the husband of her best friend Ho-jung. She begins receiving disturbing calls on her new, unregistered mobile phone. Ho-jung's five-year-old daughter, Yung-ju, becomes possessed after accidentally answering the phone, flying into fits of psychotic violence and behaving flirtatiously towards her father. Ji-won discovers that the phone originally belonged to a dead schoolgirl, Jin-hee, who was embroiled in a complex web of infertility, infidelity, jealousy and murder, and has now returned to wreak supernatural vengeance.

Background

Phone is the undoubted highlight of Ahn's filmography to date, and was a success both on home turf and internationally. It was supported through the Disney subsidiary Buena Vista Korea, demonstrating the exciting synergy then being established between eastern and western markets that has been sustained ever since. The film's story was partly based on a popular Korean urban legend about a piano-playing ghost who haunts the school where she once killed herself.

Verdict

With a female investigative journalist as a lead character and a plot predicated on the noxious effects of haunted technology, *Phone* could easily have ended up a bland *Ring* knock-off; and, admittedly, it lacks the originality and imaginative force of some of the very best films in the Asian horror canon. Nevertheless, there is plenty to enjoy here, and the production boasts pace, performances and plotting that make for a satisfying viewing experience – and one significantly more accessible to general audiences than the wilder, more outré fringes of Asian horror. By creating a sturdy (if contrived) backstory to underpin its central mystery, the film remains rooted in credible psychological realities that keep the viewer anchored and involved despite the supernatural extravagances of the ghost narrative. In addition to slick, blue-palate cinematography and spooky sound design (Beethoven's 'Moonlight Sonata' plays a pivotal role in the plot), the film owes much of its success to an extraordinary performance by Seo-woo Eun as the possessed five-year-old, Yung-ju, who takes her place alongside *The Exorcist*'s Linda Blair, *Poltergeist*'s Heather O'Rourke and *The Sixth Sense*'s Haley Joel Osment in horror cinema's pantheon of great juvenile performers. Her crooked, creepy smile is truly something to behold, and the scenes in which the child – having seemingly developed an Electra complex – behaves in a sexually suggestive way towards her own father are genuinely unsettling.

Acacia (2003)

Directed by: Ki-hyung Park
Cast: Hye-jin Shim (Mi-sook), Jin-geun Kim (Do-il), Woo-bin Moon (Jin-sung)

Story

Six-year-old Jin-sung is adopted by a middle-class couple, doctor Do-il and his wife Mi-sook, a textile artist. Mi-sook's mother is suspicious of the new arrival, and tells her daughter that it would be better to have a child of her own blood. Soon after, Mi-sook falls pregnant and gives birth to a son. Jin-sung becomes increasingly fixated on a leafless acacia tree growing in the back garden of the family home, which he claims is the reincarnation of his dead birth-mother. After an argument with Mi-sook, Jin-sung runs away from home. The relationship between husband and wife deteriorates into bitter acrimony, just as the acacia begins to grow leaves and blossom. With Jin-sung's disappearance hanging over them, the family's life is overtaken by sinister supernatural forces that seem to originate from the eponymous tree.

Background

Park's third feature was a major departure from the teen-centric, high-school shocks of *Whispering Corridors* and the sweetly romantic *Secret Tears*. On Tartan's R2 DVD release he speaks of his personal anger at the way the adoption system in Korea has broken down, pointing out that the country has one of the highest rates of farming out children overseas for adoption; these emotions are clearly reflected in his sympathetic treatment of the film's lonely young adoptee Jin-sung.

Verdict

This unusual, highly distinctive suburban horror is further confirmation of the rude health of the post-millennium Korean horror scene. Despite tipping its hat to western genre touchstones like *The Omen* (1976) and having curious echoes of David Lynch's suburban nightmare *Blue Velvet* (1986) (as well as his bizarre short *The Grandmother* [1970], in which a child 'grows' his titular relative as a kind of plant), Park's film has a whiff of genuine strangeness to it – all the more potent for its eschewal of shock tactics in favour of slow-burning enigmas.

Against the odds, the acacia tree itself proves a curiously memorable monster, shedding its gorgeous blossoms to deadly effect in a couple of unsettling set-piece scenes. The virtuoso camera shots spiralling around the tree are only some of the film's impressive visual coups: as madness grips the hapless bourgeois couple, their home becomes enmeshed in trails of carmine woollen thread, creating a sense that the house is metaphorically bleeding. But despite its flirtation with surrealism, the film remains firmly rooted in psychological realities, resolving itself into a moving parable about the immense responsibilities that adoption entails, and the pitfalls of taking an axe to the roots of an individual's identity.

A Tale of Two Sisters/Janghwa, Hongryeon (2003)

Directed by: Ji-woon Kim
Cast: Su-jung Lim (Su-mi), Geun-yung Moon (Su-yun), Jung-ah Yum (Eun-joo), Kap-su Kim (Father)

Story

Two teenagers, Su-mi and her younger sister Su-yun, return home to their father and stepmother Eun-joo after Su-mi has apparently received treatment in an asylum. Their father is cold and withdrawn. Su-yun is plagued by terrifying dreams and Su-mi becomes convinced that her sister is being abused by her stepmother. Several characters seem to experience supernatural events: Eun-joo's hand is grabbed by a ghostly figure under the sink, and Su-mi is confronted by a bleeding spectre in her bedroom. After her pet bird is murdered, Eun-joo punishes Su-yun by locking her in her mother's wardrobe. As the stakes rise, Su-mi struggles to unlock the secrets of the past that seem to have cursed her family.

Background

Kim had dealt with post-traumatic psychological damage in his previous film, *Memories*, included in the pan-Asian anthology film *Three* (the precursor to *Three... Extremes*), and was able to explore the concept at greater length in this complex reworking of a traditional Korean folktale. *Janghwa and Hongryun* ('Rose Flower and Red Lotus'), the story of a wicked stepmother persecuting her husband's daughters, had been filmed on at least five separate occasions since the silent era; the 1924 version directed by Chung-hyun Park is generally regarded as the first truly Korean film (incorporating a national story, cast, crew and director). Kim's film was the third-highest-grossing film of its year on home turf, attracting Hollywood's attention: *The Uninvited*, a Dreamworks remake directed by the Guard Brothers, was released in 2009.

Verdict

From its eerily elegant opening credits – in which CGI ripples ebb almost imperceptibly across expanses of green floral wallpaper – to its brilliantly executed series of climactic plot disclosures, Kim's film consistently proves itself worthy of admission to the ranks of the horror greats. Like *The Innocents* (1961), *The Sixth Sense* and *The Others* before it, the film is in an honourable tradition of sleight-of-hand spook stories that keep viewers teetering off-balance, before deftly ripping the rug out from under their feet. But while the storytelling is ingenious in its construction (immediately making you want to watch the film again to piece the complexities together), it is Kim's superb *mise-en-scène* that really elevates this work to classic status. The family home where most of the claustrophobic psychodrama plays out is masterfully designed, with creeping shadows seeming to leech the light and warmth from the dense assemblage of glasswork, rugs and William Morris wallpaper. These Victorian-English textures give the tale a strong Gothic resonance, and the film cunningly combines its folk-tale staples (wicked stepmother, old dark house, cursed closet) with psychoanalytical acuity, grounding events in a very human tragedy of loss, guilt and fragile minds. Kim uses some well-orchestrated shock tactics to compound the viewer's disorientation, deploying ghostly limbs and blood-soaked sacks to memorable effect; but his greatest achievement here is sustaining such a rich atmosphere of cloying unease and profound foreboding, amply fulfilling his ambition of making a horror film that is 'both beautiful and terrible'.

Old Boy (2003)

Directed by: Chan-wook Park
Cast: Min-sik Choi (Dae-su), Ji-tae Yu (Wu-jin), Hye-jung Kang (Mi-do)

Story

Salaryman Dae-su is abducted and imprisoned in an illegal private prison for 15 years. His cell resembles a hotel room with a fake window and a TV set, from which he learns that his wife has been murdered and that he is presumed to be the killer. Just when he is on the point of digging his way out with a chopstick, he is hypnotised and abruptly released. Dae-su befriends Mi-do, a young sushi chef, who later becomes his lover. A man called 'Evergreen' contacts him, claiming responsibility for his abduction and telling him he has five days to solve the mystery of his incarceration or he will kill every woman he has ever loved, including Mi-do. Dae-su tracks down the location of his prison and exacts violent retribution on his captors. He discovers that his nemesis is Wu-jin, an 'Evergreen Old Boy' from his former high school. For Dae-su, this is just the first step in fathoming the full extent of the awful revenge that Wu-jin has taken against him – an understanding that will drive him to the brink of madness and despair.

Background

This second instalment in Park's 'Vengeance Trilogy' was adapted from a Japanese *manga* created by Garon Tsuciya and Nobuaki Minegishi. It was a substantial domestic and international hit, winning the Grand Prix at the 2004 Cannes Film Festival (with jury president Quentin Tarantino as a passionate advocate) and garnering plenty of positive reviews for its imaginative direction, stylish mayhem and operatic storytelling. It gained less favourable media attention when photos of the Virginia Tech mass killer Sung-hui Cho were released, depicting him striking weapon-wielding poses that strongly echoed some of those in the film. A Steven Spielberg-helmed US remake starring Will Smith is in advanced stages of discussion.

Verdict

It's hard to imagine any actor other than the great Min-sik Choi – a Korean superstar since *Shiri* (1999) – in the role of *Old Boy*'s Dae-su Oh: with his frazzled shock of hair, glum countenance and heartbroken eyes, he's the perfect embodiment of the existential pain at the core of Park's tragic horror-thriller. He's also impressively gung-ho, taking on dozens of thugs with his claw-hammer in an epic, single-take fight sequence, and scoffing down a live octopus in a sushi restaurant. Like the protagonists in the brace of films that bookend *Old Boy* in Park's 'Vengeance Trilogy', Oh's obsessive quest for revenge eventually makes him monstrous; but, thanks to Choi's monumental performance, we never lose sight of the remaining vestiges of humanity in a character ultimately more sinned against than sinning.

Each of the films in Park's trilogy is constructed as a kind of contemporary Jacobean tragedy, in which violence, madness and death consume the feuding antagonists. But while Park's insights into the corrosive and corrupting effects of vengeance are hardly profound, his imaginative power and baroque sense of style most certainly are. *Old Boy* is a story told with tremendous cinematic panache, with Park bringing a striking sense of composition and design to almost every scene – from the sequences in Oh's *faux*-hotel-room prison cell, complete with fake window and a TV that concisely conveys the passage of years (in a flurry of images of the Hong Kong handover, Diana's death and the Twin Towers attacks), to the aforementioned mass brawl, shot like a side-scrolling, beat-'em-up video game. Park also shows a flair for grotesquery that consolidates his reputation as one of the prime movers in Asian 'extreme' cinema, ranging from squirm-inducing scenes of claw-hammer dental extractions and tongue slicing to surreal nightmare images of ants erupting from beneath Oh's skin.

The Host/Gwoemul (2006)

Directed by: Joon-ho Bong
Cast: Kang-ho Song (Gang-du), Hee-bong Byun (Hee-bong), Hae-il Park (Nam-il), Doo-na Bae (Nam-joo)

Story

Seoul's Han River is polluted by toxic chemicals poured down a laboratory sink on the orders of an American scientist. Six years later, a giant mutated monster emerges from the river and devours picnickers. The US military begin to quarantine the public, believing they've been exposed to a virus. Slobbish kiosk worker Gang-du receives a call from his schoolgirl daughter, Hyun-seo, who has been captured by the creature and stored in its lair in the sewer system. Gang-du escapes from quarantine with his father and sister (a champion archer) and they embark on a dangerous rescue mission against the backdrop of mass demonstrations against the US plans to release the anti-viral chemical 'Agent Yellow'.

Background

Bong (1969–) studied at the Korean Academy of Film Arts in the early nineties, and had already proven his directing abilities – as well as his familiarity with the idiom of US movies – on satirical comedy *Barking Dogs Never Bite* (2000) and the excellent serial-killer thriller *Memories of Murder* (2003) before helming what would become the highest-grossing Korean film of all time. To help secure the film's sizable $11 million budget, Bong apparently made a high-concept pitch by Photoshopping an image of the Loch Ness Monster onto a photo of Seoul's Han River. In the event, a pre-sale to Japan covered 40 per cent of the budget – over a third of which was spent on top-tier FX houses in New Zealand, Australia and California. In interviews, Bong has recalled watching *Godzilla* movies as a child on the American Forces Network, and *The Host* is certainly modern Asian cinema's most successful updating of the classic *kaiju eiga* formula. *The Host 2*, based on a script by leading webcomic artist Kang Full, is in the pipeline.

Verdict

The strength of *The Host* lies in its satisfying combination of the high-octane, effects-driven carnage one expects from a monster movie with its touching portrait of a dysfunctional family rallying in the teeth of adversity. The Parks, however, are no mawkish American family in the *Jurassic Park* (1993) mould: the heroism of Gang-du (played by the ubiquitous Kang-ho Song, Korea's biggest star) is generally inadvertent, and the family's near-constant bickering is played with a sense of slapstick. By keeping Hollywood sentimentality firmly at bay in these characterisations, Bong actually succeeds in making his story more moving – especially as not everyone makes it to the final reel.

Of course, this is a movie with more than just one monster: the Park family spend as much time battling the state apparatus as they do squaring up to the beast itself, and there are plenty of satirical political jabs at the way Korean authorities still squirm under the thumb of the US, who squander their resources tackling a non-existent virus and cooking up a sinister, anti-viral substance pointedly dubbed 'Agent Yellow'. *The Host*'s plot mechanics certainly align it with other Asian horrors rooted in paranoia about viral contagion – like Muroga's *Junk: Evil Dead Hunting* (2000). Ultimately though, Bong's film was always going to stand or fall on the strength of its featured creature, and it doesn't disappoint. Making one of the all-time great entrances, the beast – a 30-foot hybrid of fish and reptile with tenticular tail and slobbering maw – uncoils from the underside of a bridge and then proceeds, in broad daylight, to maraud its way clumsily along a crowded Han embankment (a banally quotidian setting for many Seoul residents), gobbling up hapless picnickers. It's this scene, above any other, that is emblematic of Korea's *Crouching Tiger, Hidden Dragon* moment of mainstream international crossover success.

HONG KONG HORROR CINEMA

Horror films were effectively outlawed in mainland China for most of the twentieth century, and consequently the vast majority of production took place in Hong Kong. This region's horror films often show a blatant disregard for the traditions of western realism, preferring instead to ransack the mythological traditions of Chinese literature and opera. A key influence was the late-seventeenth-century folk story anthology *Strange Stories from a Chinese Studio*, compiled by the wandering tutor Songling Pu. This treasure house of tales featured numerous demons, magicians, ghosts and distinctive *huli jing* ('fox spirits') that would make regular reappearances in late-twentieth-century Hong Kong fantasy and horror cinema.

Early Chinese horror films often took the form of ghostly romances – Beihai Li's *Yanzhi* (1925), now lost, set an early benchmark and was followed by the likes of *A Maid's Bitter Story* (1949) and *Ghost Woman of the Old Mansion* (1949). Han Hsiang Li's *Enchanting Shadow* (1958) was perhaps the apotheosis of this subgenre, an elegant and lyrical Songling Pu adaptation about a tragic ghost lady and her mortal lover.

Hong Kong's Cantonese dialect isolated its cinema from that of the Mandarin-speaking mainland, and by the fifties and sixties it was producing a heady mélange of martial-arts films, *wuxia* ('fantasy swordplay'), opera adaptations and melodramas. The studio Golden Harvest launched Bruce Lee and Jackie Chan onto the international stage with their flamboyant *kung fu* flicks, which proved such a phenomenon that Hammer Films were soon cashing in on the action with *The Legend of the 7 Golden Vampires* (1974), which blended an eastern Van Helsing vampire hunt with the chop-socky that had become the region's most identifiable specialty.

By the eighties and nineties, Hong Hong had become a true production powerhouse, lagging behind only India and the US in productivity. Many of the industry's principal movers-and-shakers (Jackie Chan, Sammo Hung) were versatile multi-hyphenates, juggling roles as stars, producers, directors, stuntmen and – not infrequently – pop performers. A freeform, pick-and-mix approach to genre has been the hallmark of Hong Kong cinema in the last three decades, and the majority of the region's horror films contain lashings of romance, martial arts and slapstick comedy alongside the suspense and gore. Sammo Hung's horror/comedy/*kung fu* mash-up *Encounters of the Spooky Kind* (1980) proved influential in this regard: the star-director plays a character who spends his nights in supposedly haunted properties at the behest of friends who are trying to trick him, only to end up riling the genuine ghosts who live there. Variations on the same audience-friendly formula soon appeared in the Hung-starring *The Dead and the Deadly* (1982), *Hocus Pocus* (1984) and *Encounters of the Spooky Kind 2* (1989), as well as the Hark Tsui-produced *Mr Vampire* (1985).

The latter was the key film in the region's briefly burgeoning *jiang shi* ('hopping corpse') subgenre, featuring cadavers – often vampiric – who literally hop across the screen in pursuit of their victims. Some commentators have speculated that this folkloric phenomenon originated in the practice of 'travelling a corpse', whereby Taoist priests would teach the corpses of those who passed away far from their homes to hop back there for a proper burial. Interestingly, the blood-sucking nature of Chinese vampires in these films is a relatively recent addition, betraying the influence of the western vampire tradition.

Perhaps the first Hong Kong horror production to register internationally was *A Chinese Ghost Story* (1987), which led a wave of period ghost films that included Stanley Kwan's deeply moving *Rouge* (1987) and King Hu's *Painted Skin* (1992), as well as the *Erotic Ghost Story* (1990) series. The popularity of ghost stories was later confirmed by the success of the contemporary anthology *Troublesome Night* (1997), which has spawned a jaw-dropping 18 sequels to date.

Alongside this fantasy/folklore tendency in Hong Kong horror runs a parallel trend in far more grisly serial-killer fare and lurid 'true crime' exposés. The titles speak volumes: *Human Lanterns* (1982) featured a deranged artisan using flayed flesh for his latest creations, while *Horrible High Heels* (1996) does something similar for shoes. A ratings system was set up in 1988, leading to a rash of notorious 'Category III' films in the early nineties – a designation originally designed for soft porn, but one quickly extended to gruesome home-video fare like ultra-violent prison saga *The Story of Ricky* (1992), human-meat-in-pork-bun tale *The Untold Story* (1993), serial-killer gore-fest *Dr Lamb* (1993), Billy Tang's nauseating *Red to Kill* (1994) – featuring a necrophilic serial killer targeting young girls in a mental home – and Herman Yau's *Ebola Syndrome* (1996). Spectacularly tasteless though they may be, these Cat III exploiters often showcase enough sheer low-budget invention and narrative verve to have earned their cult niche, while their influence on 'classier' productions like Fruit Chan's *Dumplings* (2004) is tangible.

The approach of the 1997 handover put the brakes on Hong Kong production, with fears of imminent curbs on expression leading to a talent exodus. Ronny Yu (*The Bride With White Hair*, 1993) was just one of several genre directors who headed Stateside, where he went on to helm *Bride of Chucky* (1998) and *Freddy vs Jason* (2003). In the event, China honoured the terms of the agreement and refrained from introducing censorship restrictions, and the Hong Kong film industry gave itself another kick-start with *Crouching Tiger,*

Hidden Dragon and *Infernal Affairs* (2002), while fresh horror voices emerged in the shape of the Pang Brothers and Chi-Leung Law. Their post-handover films display a strong Hollywood influence in their design and tone, and are certainly riper for Hollywood appropriation than the uncategorisably demented antics of Bosco Lam's *A Chinese Torture Chamber Story* (1994) – featuring spectral ghost-rapes, sex toys and archaic torture instruments – or Man-Kei Chin's *The Eternal Evil of Asia* (1995), in which a character's head is transformed by a warlock's curse into a giant, dribbling penis.

MODERN HONG KONG HORROR: ESSENTIAL VIEWING

A Chinese Ghost Story/Qiannu youhun (1987)

Directed by: Siu-Tung Ching
Cast: Leslie Cheung (Ling Choi), Joey Wong (Siu-Sihn), Ma Wu (Master Yin)

Story

Shy tax collector Ling takes shelter in an abandoned forest temple, where Siu-Sihn, a beautiful female ghost, attempts to seduce him. When he resists, the ghost falls in love with him. Unfortunately, since her death at the hands of robbers, Siu-Sihn's spirit has been in thrall to a malevolent, cross-dressing tree demon called 'The Dame', who is about to force her into marriage with the demonic Lord of the Black Mountain. Ling joins forces with the Taoist swordsman Master Yin to fight the demons. Yin opens a temporary portal to the Underworld, where Ling ventures to save Siu-Sihn from her marriage and rescue her soul. Eventually he reburies her ashes, leaving open the possibility of her future reincarnation.

Background

Based on the same Ming-era short story from Songling Pu's massively influential Grimm-style collection, *Strange Stories from a Chinese Studio*, which had already provided the basis of 1958's

Enchanting Shadow, this became a smash hit across many Asian territories and made superstars out of Leslie Cheung and Joey Wong. The pair reteamed for the brace of sequels which followed in 1990 and 1991, and the film's success also led directly to an animated adaptation and a TV series. Although Ching handled directing duties on the trilogy, some commentators have suggested that the series bears the creative fingerprints of its producer Hark Tsui, a director in his own right with some cult horror hybrids on his résumé (1979's gory thriller *The Butterfly Murders*, 1981's cannibal romp *We Are Going To Eat You* and 1983's supernatural epic *Zu: Warriors from the Magic Mountain*).

Verdict

The film's Cantonese title more literally translates as 'The Ethereal Spirit of a Beauty', which is perhaps more evocative of the romance at the heart of the tale. There is certainly a powerful erotic frisson to the ghost's infatuation with the virginal naïf Ling, and his subsequent quest to save her eternal soul by braving the horrors of the Underworld provides the film with its main narrative motor. Leslie Cheung and Joey Wong certainly make an appealing screen couple, and their highly unorthodox courtship allows the film to retain a strong emotional core, however many outrageous diversions the filmmakers concoct. These range from energetic grudge matches between rival swordsmen to outlandish SFX sequences featuring hordes of rotting, stop-motion cadavers, spectral decapitations, and the monstrous, serpentine tongue of the tree demon (a brazen lift from Raimi's *The Evil Dead*). Some of the comic moments (Siu-Sihn concealing Ling in her bath) are more effective than others (tiresome jokes about the bribing of magistrates); but with its pell-mell pacing, winning performances and impressive visuals, it's easy to appreciate why this particular formula proved so successful with the public.

Mr Vampire/Geung si sin sang (1985)

Directed by: Ricky Lau
Cast: Ching-Ying Lam (Master Ko), Siu-Ho Chin (Harry), Ricky Hui (Dan), Moon Lee (Ting-Ting)

Story

Taoist priest Master Ko and his two bungling assistants, Dan and Harry, assist with a reburial ceremony for the father of wealthy Mr Yam. They discover that the corpse is remarkably well preserved after 20 years because Mr Yam's father has become a vampire. Ko tries to bind the vampire into his coffin, but it escapes and kills Mr Yam, turning him into a vampire too. Dan has a crush on Mr Yam's daughter, Tina, and uses magic tricks to see off his equally buffoonish romantic rival, Captain Wai. When Dan falls victim to the vampire, Ko attempts various remedies, eventually managing to expel the vampire toxins. Dan, meanwhile, is seduced by a female spirit called Jade, but Ko discovers her true nature before defeating her in combat. In an epic kung-fu battle, Ko and his assistants finally destroy the vampire.

Background

Multi-talented producer Sammo Hung – one of the main creative forces driving the Hong Kong New Wave in the 1980s – teamed with director Ricky Lau to produce this domestic smash hit that put new blood into the Hong Kong horror genre, spawning four direct sequels and cementing the popularity of *jiang shi* – or 'hopping corpse' – movies. Hung had set the template for these films with *Encounters of the Spooky Kind* (1980) and *The Dead and the Deadly* (1983), which mixed Chinese folklore with daredevil martial-arts stunts, gory horror and hefty dollops of broad comedy. This subgenre inspired much affection in horror fans in the west – witness John Carpenter's *Big Trouble in Little China* (1986), or the hopping vampire in the employ of Fu Manchu featured in Kim Newman's 1992 novel *Anno Dracula*. *Mr Vampire*'s lead actor Ching-Ying Lam – formerly a stunt master on the Bruce Lee films *Fist of Fury* (1972) and *Enter the Dragon* (1973) – found himself typecast for the rest of his career as a Taoist priest in the Van Helsing mould.

Verdict

Those interested in the genealogy of *Buffy the Vampire Slayer*'s supernatural chop-socky will find plenty to pick over here. Lau's film is fantastically silly, but carried off with such verve and showmanship that it's impossible not to be swept up by its infectious energy. Having an encyclopaedia of arcane Chinese rituals and superstitions to hand would occasionally be useful, but the film is accessible enough for viewers fresh to the genre to get the hang of things: twine soaked in chicken blood is a potent weapon against vampires, and can also be used to bind them into their coffins; sacred scroll paper slapped onto the foreheads of the creatures can immobilise them; sticky uncooked rice burns their feet; a raised threshold can prevent them from hopping into a house; and holding your breath means they can't detect your presence.

As expected from a region specialising in martial arts, the stunt work and fight scenes are impressively choreographed; Master Ko's confrontation with the undead succubus bewitching his apprentice Harry – in which her head becomes temporarily detached – is a highlight. Admittedly, for western audiences some of the film's humour doesn't travel quite as well – the spectacle of the idiotic Dan donning makeup and executing ballet moves to ward off the vampire infection is too crudely conceived to raise many laughs – but Lau's hectic pacing means that the next crowd-pleasing *kung-fu* showcase is never far off.

The Untold Story/Baat sin faan dim ji yan yuk cha siu baau (1993)

Directed by: Herman Yau, Danny Lee
Cast: Anthony Wong (Chi-Hang Wong), Danny Lee (Officer Lee), Emily Kwan (Bo)

Story

A bag of human limbs is washed up on a Macau beach, triggering a police investigation. The trail leads to the Eight Immortals Restaurant, where owner Chi-Hang Wong feeds the officers pork buns. The cops discover that Chi-Hang moved to Macau from Hong Kong several years before, after killing a man over a gaming debt. They begin to suspect that Chi-Hang has murdered the restaurant's previous owner and his wife and five children, along with several employees. They torture him and place him in a prison cell with the relative of one of his victims, who proceeds to brutalise him further. Eventually, he confesses to the murders, revealing that he disposed of the bodies by putting the human meat into his pork buns.

Background

The Cantonese title of this Category III exploitation classic actually translates as *Eight Immortals Restaurant: Human Meat Roast Pork Buns*, which conveys rather more of the work's flavour than its bland English counterpart. The film's story is based on events that – while possibly apocryphal – are alleged to have taken place in the 1980s. The film's success at the box office spawned several direct rip-offs – *Human Pork Chop* (2001), *Bloody Buns* (2003) – as well as fuelling the vogue for 'true crime' films started by Cat III shocker *Dr Lamb* the previous year. Director Yau also helmed the equally notorious cannibalistic Cat III shocker *Ebola Syndrome*, as well as sections of the entertaining ghost-film omnibus *Troublesome Night* (1997).

Verdict

Anthony Wong is a fixture of Hong Kong cult cinema (*Hard Boiled* [1992], *Full Contact* [1993], *Infernal Affairs*), and it's easy to see why his bravura performance as the demented restaurateur Chi-Hang scooped him a 1993 Hong Kong Film Award for Best Actor. The character's actions are truly monstrous, and yet Wong never allows the audience to lose sight of the desperate, fragile and paranoid human being behind them. He makes it disconcertingly easy to root for this rank outsider – with his hulking frame, thick glasses and awkward grimace – who may be short-fused, paranoid, self-pitying and a compulsive cheat at Mah Jong, but is also an industrious migrant resorting to desperate measures to hold his unravelling life together. The film's deft manipulation of audience sympathies and moral compasses makes *The Untold Story* an unsettling experience. As with Norman Bates, you find yourself investing in Chi-Hang's dilemma as he improvises disposal methods for the corpses of his various victims.

The film's notoriety, however, is wholly warranted, and the sight of Chi-Hang butchering the restaurant owner's family (including his young children) requires a strong stomach; although, like many a gore-fest, the scene is so gratuitously excessive it feels more blackly comic in intent. As with other Hong Kong horror films, queasy laughs are regularly stirred into the mix (a finger dropping off a severed arm just as the police are trying to fingerprint it) along with broad humour – here revolving around the bickering, horny and largely incompetent cops bumbling their way through their investigation. The fact that they have to resort to torture and brutality to crack the case is presumably intended as a satirical swipe at the Macau police (the same group of fictional cops had also appeared in *Dr Lamb*). The film's violent shifts in register between its graphic murders and recurrent jokes about the entourage of hookers Officer Lee likes to surround himself with can certainly feel jarring to western sensibilities, although the juxtapositions make much of the mayhem feel more tongue-in-cheek by association, and therefore more palatable. Unfortunately, that certainly doesn't apply to the truly nauseating scene in which Chi-Hang terrorises and rapes a hapless waitress (before dispatching her with an eye-watering chopstick insertion), which can lay no claim to any entertainment value whatsoever – a sour moment in an otherwise satisfying slice of prime exploitation fare.

Inner Senses/Yee do hung gaan (2002)

Directed by: Chi-Leung Law
Cast: Leslie Cheung (Dr Jim Law), Karena Lam (Yan), Maggie Poon (Siu Yu)

Story

A young Hong Kong woman, Yan, is convinced that she is seeing ghosts – including those of her landlord's wife and son, who were killed in a mudslide. She is treated by psychologist Dr Jim Law, who explains to her that the spectres are products of her troubled mind, expressing the guilt she has harboured over her parents' divorce. After he engineers a cathartic meeting between Yan and her estranged parents, her mental health seems to improve, and a tentative romance starts to develop between the doctor and his charge. But Law now starts to experience visions of his own – some repressed memories, and others seemingly supernatural manifestations of his lost teenage love, Siu Yu, who threw herself off a building after a break-up triggered by his infidelity. As Siu Yu's ghost tries to propel Law towards suicide, Yan tries to help him in the same way that he helped her.

Background

Director Law made his debut with the Leslie Cheung action vehicle *Double Tap* (2000), and went on to helm the slick, organ-theft psycho-thriller *Koma* (2004), which paired *Inner Senses'* Karena Lam (formerly a singer) with *The Eye*'s Angelica Lee. *Inner Senses* was the final film made by its superstar lead Cheung, who had appeared in such Asian landmarks as *A Better Tomorrow* (1986), *A Chinese Ghost Story*, *Farewell My Concubine* (1993) and *Days of Being Wild* (1990). On 1 April 2003, he jumped from the twenty-fourth floor of Hong Kong's Mandarin Oriental Hotel, leaving a suicide note outlining his struggles with depression.

Verdict

It is impossible to watch the climactic scene of *Inner Senses*, in which Leslie Cheung's psychologically disturbed Dr Law is exhorted by the apparition of a former lover to jump from a building, without speculating about what effect making the film had on the actor's mental state: the scene would find a grotesque echo in the circumstances of his own death a few months after filming had been completed. Like James Dean in *Rebel Without a Cause* (1955), or Heath Ledger in *The Dark Knight* (2008), aspects of his final role seem to have almost leaked into his psyche, uncannily prefiguring the circumstances of his death.

Quite apart from these accidental qualities, Law's film has much to recommend it. Like the Korean masterpiece *A Tale of Two Sisters*, its ghostly visitations have psychological rather than supernatural origins, and the film gets fruitful dramatic mileage out of the ambiguous lines between the two. As with other post-handover Hong Kong films, *Inner Senses* seems determined to be able to play just as well to western audiences as eastern. Unusually for an Asian horror film, Cheung's character early on in the film rationalises the widespread belief in ghosts by analysing the culture that creates them: even though he soon starts seeing ghosts himself, his theories are ultimately vindicated rather than repudiated. Many of the chills are subtly orchestrated: in one scene, Yan's landlord explains to her that he leaves clean shoes out for his family, whom he is convinced will return to him (despite having died in a landslide); he also talks of cooking extra food for his wife so that she can gain weight. Elsewhere, Law is content to raid the J-Horror box of tricks for a scene in which the ghost of Dr Law's schoolgirl lover rises from the floor with a ghastly creaking sound, her childish giggling mixed into the soundtrack to unnerving effect.

Dumplings/Gaau ji (2004)

Directed by: Fruit Chan
Cast: Ling Bai (Mei), Miriam Yeung (Mrs Li), Tony Leung (Mr Li)

Story

Wealthy former actress Mrs Li is desperate to revitalise her relationship with her husband of 15 years, who she knows is having an affair with his masseuse. She visits Aunt Mei, a local chef, who cooks her some special dumplings that she claims have rejuvenating qualities. Mei is 64, but has the body of a woman half her age. Mrs Li is fully aware that the special ingredients Mei uses are aborted foetuses, imported from the mainland abortion clinic where Mei used to work. Mei performs a black-market abortion on a schoolgirl who has been raped by her father. The dumplings seem to do the trick, and the married couple make love. Mr Li learns of his wife's visits to Mei, and visits her himself, eating her dumplings and having sex with her. The schoolgirl later dies from her abortion, and her mother kills her husband, leading to a police raid on Mei's apartment which forces her to flee back to the mainland. Mrs Li learns that the masseuse is going to have her husband's child and bribes her to abort it. She makes the foetus into dumplings and eats them.

Background

Although clearly always planned as a full feature, a shorter cut of Chan's film first appeared in Applause's impressive pan-Asian anthology *Three... Extremes* (2004), where it was partnered with Chan-wook Park's *Cut* and Takashi Miike's *Box*. The shorter version retains much of the main plot, but excludes the masseuse's pregnancy and subsequent abortion; instead, Mrs Li ends up consuming her *own* aborted foetus. The film was adapted by Lillian Lee (*Rouge, Farewell My Concubine*) from her own short story, and was apparently based on reports that emerged in the mid-nineties from Shenzhen in mainland China about hospital staff eating aborted foetuses as a nutritional supplement. *Dumplings* was produced by Applause co-founder Peter Chan, who helmed a segment of 2002's original *Three* omnibus, and directed by indie social satirist Fruit Chan (*Made in Hong Kong*, 1997).

Verdict

Shot by master cinematographer Chris Doyle, *Dumplings* is one of the most visually ravishing of Asian horrors – entirely appropriate for a film concerned with the lure of surface appearances. The cooking sequences – in which Ling Bai's perky Aunt Mei lovingly prepares her rejuvenating dumplings – are so enticing to watch, and the final products so succulent in appearance that it's *almost* possible to overlook the nature of the 'special filling' that makes them so potent. Shrewdly, director Chan doesn't waste time trying to generate suspense about the nature of these ingredients, and Mrs Li is always aware that Mei is a procurer of aborted foetuses; this allows his film to focus its satirical bite on the culture that has birthed such an apparently monstrous practice in a way that Jonathan Swift would have thoroughly approved of. It's a testament to the richness of the material here that the film can simultaneously function as a critique of China's one-child policies, an indictment of Hong Kong's out-of-control consumerism (particularly among the moneyed middle classes, here literally eating the poor), a rebuke to the superstitions of 'traditional' Chinese medicine and a more general attack on human vanity and a society's obsession with youth. While some of the Cat III films portraying cannibalism (*The Untold Story, Ebola Syndrome*) are far more graphic, it would take a stomach of iron not to squirm at some of the sequences Chan serves up here – especially when accompanied by nauseatingly evocative dialogue discussing textures and nutritional value ('The best are those in the fifth or sixth month, [...] covered by a layer of creamy fat. The colours are defined. You can even see the cranium!'). The leads all give spot-on performances, with Miriam Yeung particularly impressive as the society lady both ruthless enough to resort to such extreme measures to reclaim her husband, and vulnerable enough to need to do so in the first place. Ling Bai, who plays the sexy sexagenarian Aunt Mei, is a fixture of Hollywood films, including *The Crow* (1994), *Red Corner* (1997) and *Anna and the King* (1999).

THAI TERRORS

In the mid-nineties, the Thai film industry was hanging on by its fingernails, reeling under the twin assaults of television and Hollywood imports and only managing to produce a handful of films each year. Domestic filmmakers realised they needed to raise their game to attract audiences and investment (especially after the Asian financial crisis), and in 1997 a group of ex-ad directors did just that: Ratanaruang Pen-ek's *Fun Bar Karaoke* and Nimibutr Nonzee's *Dang Birley and the Young Gangsters* spearheaded a 'Thai New Wave' with international presence and domestic box office. Nonzee followed up this success with the ghost film *Nang Nak* (1999), which gained synergy from the simultaneous J- and K-Horror booms and established Thai horror as a viable genre. The fruits came in quick succession: *Bangkok Haunted* (2001), The Pang Brothers' *The Eye* (2002), Nonzee's contribution to the anthology film *Three* (2002), *Shutter* (2004) and the *Fatal Attraction*/black magic shocker *Art of the Devil* (2004). There was even a remake of Nakagawa's *Hell* called *Narok* (2005).

As in other Asian countries, there has also been a vogue in Thailand for genre-bending horror-comedies. Director Sippapak Yuthlert (1966–) incorporated references to *The Exorcist* and *Audition* into his blackly comic *Rahtree: Flower of the Night* (2003), the tale of a jilted girl taking revenge on her playboy lover, while *SARS Wars* (2004) is a garish, no-holds-barred zombie/comedy hybrid. 2004's *Garuda* was a riff on both Larry Cohen's *Q: The Winged Serpent* (1982) and

The Host, involving the discovery of the titular mythical bird divinity (Thailand's national symbol) in the Bangkok subway system. Some are frankly bizarre: Ru-Tar Rotar's freakishly fantastic *Ginseng King* (1989) involves a boy trying to outwit an evil three-headed king to save his mother, who has been bitten by a blood-sucking Nazi zombie.

Monsters from Thai folk culture crop up in other films. Yuthlert's 2006 horror-romance *Krasue Valentine* drew on the myth of the *krasue* – the floating, disembodied head of a vampiric female ghost, trailing its oesophagus behind – which had also been the subject of the 2002 Thai horror *Demonic Beauty*. This creature appears in other South East Asian cultures – its Indonesian variant is known as a *penanggalen*. Chatemee Haeman's comic-horror *Body Jumper* (2001) features a *pop*, a liver-devouring spirit capable of possessing people. In this entertaining variant, the entity (a ghostly, clawed crone) is exorcised from a village in 1930s Siam, only to be reawakened 70 years later by some students working on a rural development project. The spirit takes up residence in the body of a nubile girl, who proceeds to seduce her male admirers as a prelude to ripping out their livers.

Thai cinema, like that of South Korea, has benefited from the decline of Hong Kong cinema following the handover. Thailand's relative liberalism has led to an influx of film industry professionals formerly based in Hong Kong. The industry's newfound vitality was reflected with the launch of the Bangkok Film Festival in 1998 (later superseded by the Bangkok International Film Festival in 2002).

THE PANG BROTHERS

Danny and Oxide Pang (1965–), born Hong Kong Chinese, became poster boys for the cross-cultural energies sweeping around the East Asian film scene in the late-nineties. The twins' *modus operandi* apparently involves directing scenes independently of each other, each shooting on different days after joint discussion and planning. Aside from their horror work, the brothers have also co-directed several thriller and martial arts fantasies, and both have also directed solo projects. The brothers both began their careers in post-production – a fact that would stand them in good stead when they started directing. Oxide emigrated to Thailand in 1992 to work as a colourist, while Danny built up his credentials as an editor in Hong Kong (assignments included 2002's *Infernal Affairs*, remade by Scorsese in 2006 as *The Departed*). The success of Nonzee's *Dang Birley* opened the gates for Thai film production, and Oxide seized the opportunity by directing the *karma*-themed *Who Is Running?* (1997), which Danny cut for him. They made their co-directing debut with the impressive Thai hitman thriller *Bangkok: Dangerous* (1999), remade almost a decade later with Nicholas Cage. Oxide then collaborated with Praesangeam Pisut on the anthology *Bangkok Haunted* (2001), after which the brothers reunited for their big horror hit *The Eye* (2002) – a Thai/Hong Kong co-production that proved to modern audiences that the Japanese didn't have the monopoly on scary oriental ghosts. This hit spawned two sequels which they also helmed – *The Eye 2* (2004) and *The Eye 10* (2005). Their next horror offering was *Re-cycle* (2006), the story of a writer (played by Angelica Lee, Oxide's partner and star of *The Eye*) who starts to experience supernatural scenarios that she'd outlined in a deleted draft of her novel. Their English-language debut *The Messengers*, a Sam Raimi-produced supernatural thriller set on an idyllic sunflower farm in North Dakota, followed in 2007.

Key Horror Works

Bangkok Haunted (2001), *The Eye* (2002), *Abnormal Beauty* (2004), *The Eye 2* (2004), *The Eye 10* (2005), *Re-cycle* (2006), *The Messengers* (2007)

THAI TERRORS: ESSENTIAL VIEWING

Nang Nak (1999)

Directed by: Nimibutr Nonzee
Cast: Kraibutr Winai (Mak), Jaroenpura Intira (Nak)

Story

In rural Thailand, Mak is forced to leave his pregnant wife, Nak, in order to fight the Burmese in the Chiang Toon War. After narrowly escaping death, he returns to his wife and child. The villagers know that Nak actually died in childbirth, and realise that Mak has been bewitched by his wife's ghost. Desperate to remain with her husband, the ghost kills those who try to warn him. Having burned down Mak's home, the villagers call in a Buddhist exorcist. Eventually, Mak realises that he has been living in an abandoned and decrepit house. Nak finally agrees to leave Mak in peace. The exorcist cuts out the centre of Nak's forehead, and has a brooch fashioned from it.

Background

Nonzee's film is based on a nineteenth-century folk legend that holds a hallowed place in Thai culture. The story had been a stalwart of Thai cinema since the silent era – an equally celebrated version, *Mae Nak Pra Kanong*, was released in 1958, while more recently British filmmaker Mark Duffield directed *Ghost of Mae Nak* (2005).

An opera version, written by the Thai composer Sucharitkul Somtow, premiered in 2003. In Bangkok's Suan Lang district there is a shrine dedicated to the loyal ghost and her child, to which the devout and the curious make offerings of clothes, toys, candles and garlands.

Verdict

Fully deserving of its place at the cornerstone of the late-nineties 'Thai New Wave', Nonzee's ravishingly beautiful film is truly poignant, harnessing the pathos of other Asian horrors about men folk bewitched by phantom lovers (*Tales of Ugetsu, Kwaidan, A Chinese Ghost Story*) but given a distinctively sensual Thai feel with its lush jungle setting. Some of the credit must fall to cinematographer Kittikhun Nattawut (whose sumptuous work on the Nonzee-produced *Tears of the Black Tiger* (2000) is also worth seeking out), but performances and pacing are also well judged, and the director manages to create some unnerving moments – like the iconic scene in which the husband sees Nak's arm stretch to unnatural lengths to retrieve some fallen fruit beneath their hut.

The Eye/Jian Gui (2002)

Directed by: The Pang Brothers
Cast: Angelica Lee (Ka-Man Wong), Lawrence Chou (Lo Wah), Chutcha Rujinanon (Chiu Wai-Ling), Candy Lo (Mun's sister)

Story

Hong Kong concert violinist Ka-Man receives cornea grafts to restore the sight she lost in childhood. She is placed in the care of psychotherapist Lo Wah, the nephew of her eye surgeon, who tries to help her make visual sense of the world. Soon, however, she is seeing ghosts of the recently dead and experiencing visions of an unfamiliar room. She realises that every time she looks in the mirror, she is seeing the face of a different woman. With Lo's help, Ka-Man discovers that the transplant donor was Ling, a girl from a Thai village. Together they head to Thailand to investigate the circumstances of Ling's death and solve the mystery of Ka-Man's disturbing visions.

Background

The UK trailer for *The Eye* rather cheekily asserts that the film is 'based on a true story', which rather beggars belief. However, the Pangs have claimed that they were inspired to write the film's screenplay after reading an article many years before in a Hong Kong newspaper reporting on the suicide of a teenager shortly after she had received a corneal transplant. Whatever the origins of the tale, its legacy is not in dispute, with the Pangs themselves having notched up two sequels: *The Eye 2*, about the ghost of a suicide trying to reincarnate herself through a pregnant woman's child, and *The Eye 10*, which explores ten different methods of seeing the dead. The film has also been remade twice – in India as *Naina* (2005) and in Hollywood as the Jessica Alba-vehicle *The Eye* (2008).

Verdict

Transplanted body parts have a tendency to misbehave in horror films – from the criminal brain of Frankenstein's monster through Oliver Stone's *The Hand* (1981) and Eric Red's *Body Parts* (1991), to the pair of peepers inherited by Ka-Man in the Pangs' modern horror classic. Replacing a character's eyes is a neat – albeit derivative (*Blink*, 1994) – conceit, and even if the notion of 'seeing dead people' inevitably packs less punch a few years on from *The Sixth Sense*, it still gives the brothers the opportunity to deploy the full range of their impressive technical skills on this Thai/Hong Kong co-production in the service of some ultra-stylish, nerve-jangling set-pieces. By preserving an exceptionally shallow focus, the cinematography forces the viewer to share Ka-Man's visual disorientation, with blurred forms moving eerily beyond the limits of her eyesight. This visual technique – combined with tight editing and discreet digital effects – helps deliver a number of genuinely unnerving moments throughout the first half of the film, as Ka-Man finds herself besieged by apparitions of the recently deceased, who are then escorted to the afterworld by shadowy wraiths.

Unfortunately, the film's narrative cogs start to creak noisily during the Thai-set section of the film, with the belated introduction of a weighty, *Ring*-influenced backstory. Consequently, the film resolves rather unsatisfyingly, with coherence being thrown to the wind in favour of some high-octane pyrotechnics. Nevertheless, a sympathetic lead performance from Malaysian-Taiwanese singer Angelica Lee (later engaged to Oxide Pang) keeps the audience engaged in her plight, and there are enough cherishable scares on offer here for *The Eye* to have earned its place at the top table of modern Asian horror.

Shutter/Sutter kodtid winyan (2004)

Directed by: Pisanthanakun Banjong, Wongpoom Parkpoom
Cast: Ananda Everingham (Tun), Thongmee Natthaweeranuch (Jane), Achita Sikamana (Natre)

Story

After a drunken evening, Bangkok photographer Tun and his fiancée Jane run over a girl in their car and flee the scene. Tun soon starts seeing a ghostly figure through his camera viewfinder, which also starts appearing in the prints he develops. They discover that no body was found at the accident scene. Meanwhile, several of Tun's friends start to commit suicide. Jane becomes convinced that the disappearance of Tun's ex-girlfriend Natre is somehow connected to the haunting, and discovers that the ghost may be motivated by a dark incident in Tun's past.

Background

Shutter was the debut feature of co-directors and co-writers Banjong and Parkpoom. Both had made a couple of shorts apiece that had performed well on the international festival circuit – especially Parkpoom's ode to sexual awakening, *In the Eyes* (2003), and Banjong's *Colorblind* (2002). The latter had also worked as a film critic for the Thai entertainment magazine *Starpics*, and as an assistant director on TV commercials. *Shutter* was Thailand's biggest box-office hit in its year of release and also made a splash in Singapore, Malaysia, the Philippines and Brazil. Spurred by their success, the directors reteamed for another horror offering, *Alone* (2007) – a conjoined-twins fable featuring a dual role for Thai-German pop singer Marsha Wattanapanich (now also in line for a US remake) – and each went on to direct a segment of the Thai portmanteau horror *4bia* (2008). *Shutter* itself underwent a Tamil makeover in 2007 as *Sivi*, before a US remake appeared the following year, helmed by Japanese director Masayuki Ochiai, director of the J-Horror Theatre instalment *Infection* (2004).

Verdict

Like several of its Asian horror predecessors (*Ring, Phone, One Missed Call, Pulse*), *Shutter*'s plotting hinges on haunted technology – in this case, Polaroids and a retro SLR camera rather than a modern digital model (which would naturally provide less opportunity for supernatural shenanigans in the darkroom). But if the film's initial premise seems a little tired, it soon develops into an intriguing story of repressed guilt (there are echoes here of Nakagawa's *Hell*, which also opens with a hit-and-run incident) that boasts plenty of solid scares and a final reel that snaps the last pieces of its narrative jigsaw satisfyingly into place. Particularly impressive is a scene in which the ghost creates a sequence of instant photos that the heroine Jane is able to use like a pre-cinematic 'flicker book' to uncover her boyfriend's dark secret, and the revelation of why Tun has been experiencing neck pain since the car accident. The vengeful Natre is in the mould of a classic, lank-haired *onryou*, although her relentless pursuit of Tun along ceilings, down fire escapes and even alongside a speeding vehicle makes her one of the most frightening of the post-Sadako Asian spooks. Hell-bent on driving her former male tormentors to suicide and insanity, she tears another sizable chunk out of the soft underbelly of traditional masculine complacency.

EAST GOES WEST:
LOST IN TRANSLATION?

Back in the era of *Godzilla*, Hollywood executives who saw western commercial prospects in an eastern genre film would acquire the original and then bowdlerise it in any way they saw fit: trim anything that didn't 'travel' well, rustle up some explanatory intertitles, add some (frequently slipshod) dubbing and – on occasion – film some extra footage with a waning star (Raymond Burr, for instance) before rush-releasing with a minimal acknowledgement of the source.

Nowadays, of course, Hollywood's remake machine has adopted a different – but equally condescending – approach in its accommodation of a mass audience that is resistant to subtitles and dubbing and tends to back away from films lacking recognisable stars. Even if one is not a self-proclaimed 'cultist', jealously protective of the exclusive niche status of Asian horror, it is easy to feel warily ambivalent about these remakes. On the one hand, they inevitably raise the international profile of the original eastern horrors, ensuring a greater awareness of the source inspirations and extending their distribution. On the other, the Hollywood studios that acquire the remake rights frequently withhold the release of the Asian originals so as not to damage the remake's box-office potential. This means that audiences – particularly in the US – often experience the Asian originals after seeing the remakes, inevitably diluting their impact. After its acquisition by DreamWorks, Nakata's *Ring* was held off the market to clear the way for Gore Verbinski's remake – by which time multiplex audiences had, in any case, already been exposed to the derivative scares of *fear dot com* (2002). Meanwhile, Miramax shelled out for Kurosawa's *Pulse* after its 2001 Cannes screening and shelved it until releasing it briefly in the US in late 2005 to whip up enthusiasm for the remake.

Verbinski's *The Ring* (2002) proved a box-office smash (grossing almost $250 million worldwide, and incidentally making more money in Japan than Nakata's original), opening the floodgates for a torrent of US remakes that has continued to the present day. The critical reception of the majority of these films has been generally negative, with some bemoaning the manner in which the subtleties of the originals are jettisoned in favour of cruder storytelling, and others pointing out that they fail on the level of simply being less frightening. In addition to the frequent geographic relocation of the stories and the addition of American stars (usually ascendant young actresses), several other common strategies have emerged. Generally, the slow-burn pacing of the Asian originals is sharply ramped up, combined with an increase in the number of scare-jolts administered to the audience, while the low-fi special effects of some of the originals are usually replaced with CGI-enhanced spookery. But more significantly, while Asian horror films are content to leave certain mysteries unexplained, or for the narratives and character motivations to retain a core of ambiguity, the remakes tend to add layers of exposition that attempt to rationalise – and thereby contain – their supernatural stories.

Nowhere is this more evident than in *The Ring*, which adds numerous plot details to Nakata's enigmatic original. The cursed video at the centre of the story now contains a sequence of highly art-directed images ('very film school', as the heroine's ex-partner drily remarks), including a ladder, a tree, a centipede, a woman in a mirror and a 'ring' of light which are all painstakingly explained as the film progresses. Also included is a rationale for the curse's seven-day timeframe, and an explanation of how the video was recorded in the first place (Samara, the film's Sadako equivalent, has the ability to project nightmare images from her mind). All of these modifications feel like attempts to render the sheer weirdness of the Nakata original into something more palatable to a western mindset preoccupied with easily digested gobbets of information. Certainly, the film has creditable aspects: Naomi Watts – in her first starring role since her breakthrough in Lynch's *Mulholland Dr.* (2001) – acquits herself well in the lead, while the Seattle locations and the addition of a horse ranch to the island location work well. It says a lot about the enterprise, though, that the film's most memorable scene – in which a suicidal stallion runs amok on a ferry – has no analogue in the original, while the reworking of Nakata's celebrated sequence in which Samara crawls jerkily out of the TV set is marred by CGI overkill.

In August 2002, during the Japanese public holiday of *O-Bon*, the Festival of the Dead, a 'funeral' was held for Sadako in Tokyo, a gimmick which seemed designed to symbolise the handing of the franchise's reins to Samara and her US creators. The American remake rights for *Ring*, *Ju-On: The Grudge* and several other Asian hits were brokered by the Korean-American producer Roy Lee's Vertigo Entertainment, and Lee took an Executive Producer credit on several of the upcoming remakes for various different studios. Sam Raimi and Rob Tapert set up Ghost House Pictures specifically to remake foreign horrors for US audiences. Recognising that it would be hard to come up with a film as nerve-jangling as the original *Ju-On: The Grudge*, they hired the original's director Takashi Shimizu to deliver *The Grudge* (2004), a (sometimes shot-for-shot) English-language 'cover version' of the Japanese hit. Shimizu had already mined the material several times already with his V-Cinema versions and the Japanese sequel, and his scares in the remake hit the mark with machine-tooled precision. The US version wisely retains the Tokyo setting and the same haunted house, along with actors Takako Fuji and Yuya Ozeki in their indelible roles as the mother and son spooks Kayako and Toshio. *Buffy's* Sarah Michelle Gellar adds some star wattage, although her screen time is limited by the fragmented, episodic structure that remains the franchise's hallmark (a structure that allows Shimizu to serve up a doozy of an opening scene in which Bill Pullman's character calmly throws himself off a balcony). More solid support is provided by Grace Zabriskie (*Twin Peaks*) as the frail invalid attended to by Gellar's carer and Ryo Ishibashi (*Audition, Suicide Club*) as the detective investigating the murders. As with *The Ring*, redundant CGI are added that somehow prove less effective than the low-tech inventiveness of the source, although the unnerving simplicity of Toshio's demonic cat yowl remains intact – no doubt helping the film rack up a worldwide gross approaching $200 million. Arguably, this 'cover' now plays out as a reactionary culture-clash tale in which blameless ex-pat westerners are menaced by inscrutable and seemingly motiveless – but undeniably malevolent – oriental ghosts, stripping Kayako of some of the sympathy that the original built up for her as an abused wife.

If the Shimizu signing was a safe bet, the hiring of Brazilian director Walter Salles for the 2005 remake of Nakata's *Dark Water* was more of a gamble: his track record was in character dramas steeped in social realism, like *Central Station* (1998) and *The Motorcycle Diaries* (2004), rather than in the horror genre. But, in the event, he delivered arguably the best Asian horror remake to date – albeit one that significantly tinkers with the mechanics of the original. Jennifer Connelly is splendidly brittle as Dahlia Williams (the Yoshimi role), a fragile single mother locked into an acrimonious custody battle with her husband (Dougray Scott) over her daughter, Ceci. The leaking apartment that mother and daughter move to is situated in a Brutalist block on Roosevelt Island – a short cable-car ride from Manhattan, but very much a world apart. This grimly depressing location is one of the film's aces, and Salles gives his cinematographer, Affonso Beato, and production designer, Thérèse DePrez, plenty of scope to build up a sense of dank oppression and clammy claustrophobia, based on a colour scheme that seems keyed to the hue of a rotting cadaver. Salles ropes in several dependable character actors to flesh out some of the minor parts: John C Reilly nearly steals the show as the smarmy estate agent browbeating Dahlia into signing the lease, while Pete Postlethwaite and Tim Roth give memorable turns as a shifty caretaker and a lawyer on the skids.

Thanks to its high-calibre performances and intelligent visual design, this remake certainly delivers as an effective and emotionally engaging thriller – even despite Salles' premature introduction of the water tower at the crux of the mystery. But it's clear that Salles and his screenwriter, Rafael Yglesias, have opted to largely jettison the supernatural eeriness of the original in favour of a more purely psychological reading: this allows the film to fully indulge its themes of mental vulnerability, maternal abandonment and the craving for love at the expense of the original's more unsettling embrace of the uncanny and otherworldly. As Mark Kermode noted in a piece for *Sight & Sound*, the film seems influenced more by the Polanski of *Repulsion* (1965) and *The Tenant* (1976) than by more overtly supernatural films like *The Haunting*, or – indeed – the original *Dark Water*. Some of the most telling changes to the source occur at the film's ending. Nakata's horrific, lift-set climax, in which Yoshimi realises she is cradling a corpse-girl, is replaced by a diluted encounter with the petulant ghost-girl, Natasha, in Dahlia's living room. Omitting Nakata's scene in which the teenage Ikuko returns to the apartment and has an unsettling encounter with her long-absent mother, the remake substitutes a more reassuring epilogue which implies that the ghost-child will never supplant Ceci in her mother's affections. Salles' remake, then, has much to recommend it on its own terms, but is unlikely to generate the restless nightmares of Nakata's original.

Nakata himself had his first chance to jump on the Americanisation bandwagon when Verbinski passed on the chance to direct *The Ring Two* (2005). This was not, in fact, a remake of the director's own *Ring 2*, but a freshly concocted storyline (following on from the events of the Verbinski remake) in which Naomi Watts's Rachel attempts to save her son, Aidan, from possession by the vengeful Samara, who has pursued them from Seattle to a provincial Oregon coastal town. The cursed videotape of the original makes a brief appearance in the opening sequence, but is then wisely dropped from the narrative in favour of an intriguing exploration of parent-child bonds that is actually closer to the spirit of the original *Dark Water* than the Salles remake. Water imagery is very much to the fore: Rachel discovers that Samara's birth-mother, Evelyn (a sly cameo from Sissy Spacek, whose Carrie White was an iconic possessed child of an earlier era) attempted to drown her daughter as a perverse gesture of love – an impulse that Rachel is disturbingly compelled to replicate to try and save Aidan. Like Jennifer Connelly, Naomi Watts wrings plenty of nuance out of a meaty role that dances along the line of psychological instability (here manifesting as outright child abuse) before modulating into a fierce resolve: her climactic snarl of "I'm not your fucking mummy!" should give even the implacable Samara pause – although the announcement of *The Ring Three* after this film notched up over $160 million worldwide indicates that she may have unfinished business. This film certainly deserves credit for trying to take this now truly international franchise into fresh territory – although a bizarre scene in which Rachel and Aidan are attacked in their car by a herd of CGI stags, perhaps intended as a homage to *The Omen*, is probably an innovation too far.

The uncovering of Samara's origins adds a legitimate layer of interest to *Ring*'s ever-expanding parallel mythologies, but the same can hardly be said for the fleshing out of vengeful Kayako's backstory in *The Grudge 2* (2006), which smacks of a desperate attempt to add interest to a franchise that has definitely passed its sell-by date. Sony once again signed up Takashi Shimizu, although this film is not a direct remake of his earlier *Ju-On: The Grudge 2*. The format remains intact, though, with three separate storylines mixed in around a convoluted timeframe. Sarah Michelle Gellar's Karen may have survived the earlier film (burning down the haunted house in the process), but this time sticks around just long enough to justify her name on the billing before the reins are taken up by her sister Aubrey (Amber Tamblyn), who tracks down Kayako's exorcist mother and uncovers some distinctly unsatisfying origins of 'The Curse'. A second storyline involves three students at a Tokyo international school who ill-advisedly venture into the charred husk of the Saeki house, while a third strand is set in Chicago (presumably laying the groundwork for a Stateside shift in the plots of future instalments). Admittedly, Shimizu is still more than capable of engineering some frightening moments – scenes in a photographic darkroom and a school principal's office are highlights – but the sense of diminishing returns is overwhelming (a series of Internet 'webisodes' entitled *Tales from the Grudge* were even created in advance of the film's release, mining the same seam). 'There can be no end to what has started,' opines Kiyoshi's mother; for the sake of Asian horror's reputation, we can only hope she's wrong.

Some remakes seem more like desecrations than respectful reinterpretations. The 2006 remake of Kiyoshi Kurosawa's *Pulse* was originally planned as a Wes Craven project, but in the event was helmed by promo director Jim Sonzero, with Craven retaining a co-writing credit. The Japanese original was the antithesis of a slick, machine-tooled shocker, clearly far less interested in plot and characterisation than in its ambitious metaphysical speculations; it memorably conjured a gnawing sense of the anomie and spiritual exhaustion at the core of an atomised urban world, in which new technologies isolated people rather than helping them connect. Predictably, the Romania-shot Hollywood retooling dispenses with the (admittedly confusing) ambiguities of the original and creates a tidy backstory involving a virus that – when inadvertently distributed by an enterprising hacker – unlocks a portal to the afterworld ('There are some frequencies we were never meant to find,' as the tagline intones). The skimpily attired, eye-candy cast (including *Veronica*

Mars' Kristen Bell and *Lost's* Ian Somerhalder) are ill-equipped to convey much of a sense of existential angst, and Sonzero ramps up Kurosawa's meditative cool to a pell-mell pace. He replicates the staging of Kurosawa's principal shocks (including the single-shot tower suicide, the weird webcam visions and a spook advancing jerkily from the shadows) and adds a couple of eye-catching set-pieces himself – including a contorted ghost emerging from a dryer in a basement laundry and the heroine's startling, CGI vision of a huge writhing pile of bodies as a ghost drains her life force. The gloomily subdued visual style of the original is replaced with an artily desaturated treatment familiar from Verbinski's *The Ring.* The remake performed poorly at the box office (around $30 million worldwide), but still spawned a couple of direct-to-video sequels – *Pulse 2: Afterlife* (2008) and *Pulse 3: Invasion* (2008), both written and directed by Joel Soisson – while Sonzero went on to direct sequences for computer game *Resident Evil 5.*

Takashi Miike's *One Missed Call* (2003) has remained his most mainstream project to date and, despite its conspicuous debts to *Ring* (characters receiving phone messages from the near future playing back the sound of their imminent demise), managed to orchestrate enough inventively murderous *coup-de-grâces* and elaborate narrative red-herrings (involving Münchausen syndrome by proxy) to make it a slick and highly watchable piece of entertainment. Warner Brothers' 2008 remake somehow manages to turn even this multiplex-friendly material into something dull and enervating. Ed Burns phones in a staggeringly flat performance as a detective helping Shannyn Sossamon's psychology student get to the bottom of the string of deaths before they too receive a fatal missed call. French director Eric Valette (*Maléfique*, 2002) manages to fluff some of the original's most memorable set-pieces, with the sequence featuring the live TV exorcism show *American Miracles* (presided over by an unctuous Ray Wise, once again dragging around his *Twin Peaks* baggage) a pale shadow of its distinctly more unnerving

Japanese counterpart. An early death scene at a railway bridge is also confusingly staged, while Miike's blackly comic lift-shaft demise is jettisoned in favour of a shrapnel impalement from a gas explosion. In these scenes, the remake wears its debt to the *Final Destination* franchise a little too openly (where will the danger come from?), while sequences in which cursed characters catch glimpses of ghosts with deformed faces on the streets are lifted straight out of *Jacob's Ladder*. Miike's intriguingly ambiguous ending is also replaced with a clichéd, standard-issue 'twist'.

The remake rights to the Pang Brothers' *The Eye* were snapped up by Tom Cruise's production company, who eventually repackaged it in 2008 into a vehicle for Jessica Alba under the direction of French duo David Moreau and Xavier Palud (responsible for tense home-invasion thriller *Them* [2006]). Alba is surprisingly adequate as the blind violinist originally played by Angelica Lee – her well-publicised music lessons, Braille tutorials and time with a white cane evidently of some use – although Alessandro Nivola and Parker Posey struggle to flesh-out the underdeveloped roles of neural specialist and doting sister. Some of the transplant is a success: the film's third-act transition to rural Mexico is a neat analogue to the original's use of a Thai village as the source of the horror. Shame, then, that the film rather slavishly follows most of the Pangs' original sequences, but still manages to blunt some of the best scares by rushing the pace and failing to match the bravura tricksiness of some of the Pangs' visual coups. Sops to rationalism come in the form of babble about 'cellular memory' (the capacity of living tissue to remember experiences), while the fact that Alba's character didn't receive a transplant earlier is explained away by an observation that 'stem cell research changed the game'. Unfortunately, the snarling spectres who drag the deceased off to the netherworld have a distinctly third-hand feel (the Pangs' versions were emotionless emissaries), and the original's fiery climax has been reductively reconceived, replacing the resigned despair of a Cassandra unable to prevent history repeating itself with a comfortingly facile – and far less chilling – moment of redemptive clarity.

The remake of another Thai shocker, *Shutter*, was actually the Hollywood debut of Japanese director Masayuki Ochiai (*Infection*). The story is given a trans-Pacific retool, with Joshua Jackson and Rachael Taylor playing a Brooklyn photographer and his new wife who relocate to Tokyo for a working honeymoon. The film manages to squeeze some mileage from the characters' sense of dislocation in a foreign city and has one effective set-piece lit entirely by bursts of flash from Jackson's camera as the vengeful Megumi advances towards him. Generally, though, Ochiai cleaves closely to Banjong and Parkpoom's original, boosting the yuck factor with a gory death in which a victim's eye is gouged out through a camera's viewfinder and a scene in which Jackson's character is choked by Megumi's serpentine tongue. Reputedly, the film has made a worldwide gross of $44 million from an $8-million budget, giving the lie to the notion that the public appetite for Asian horror remakes has dried up, even for a film with such uniformly unappealing characters.

Kiefer Sutherland used one of his filming breaks from his TV series *24* to star in *Mirrors* (2008), Alexandre Aja's remake of Sung-ho Kim's 2003 Korean supernatural thriller *Into the Mirror*. His character – an ex-NYPD detective and recovering alcoholic reduced to working as a security guard in a burned-out department store – cleaves fairly closely to the Jack Bauer template: dogged by dark deeds from his past (in this case, shooting his partner), he is still desperate to rebuild his dysfunctional family. When the store's mirrors take on a malevolent life of their own, he must race to uncover the building's dark secrets before he and his loved ones are possessed by their reflections. Frenchman Aja proved his horror chops with the intense Gallic gore of *Switchblade Romance* (2003) and ramps up the graphic violence of Kim's original (one character gamely rips off her own jaw). But after a gruesome opening sequence in which the store's original night watchman dies after his sinister reflection slashes his throat,

Aja gets diminishing returns from the scare-potential of reflective surfaces, and is quickly hamstrung by the film's contrivances and the underlying risibility of its premise. Despite being less faithful to its source than some recent Asian horror remakes (it adds an entire backstory about a demonic possession in a mental hospital), *Mirrors* fails to make any modifications that improve on the original.

Clearly, the well of Asian horror is deep and dark, and it seems that Hollywood will keep returning there for recyclable templates for the foreseeable future: 2009 saw the release of *The Uninvited*, a remake by the Guard Brothers of *A Tale of Two Sisters*, while remakes of *Inner Senses*, *Old Boy* and *Death Note* are just some of the others in the pipeline, along with further instalments of *The Ring* and *The Grudge*. It's worth bearing in mind that, in recent years, this cultural pillaging has gone hand-in-hand with Hollywood's cannibalisation of one of its own 'golden ages' of horror cinema, with a stream of remakes of classic slashers, spook stories and survival horrors like *The Hills Have Eyes* (1977 and 2006), *The Texas Chainsaw Massacre* (1974 and 2003), *The Amityville Horror* (1979 and 2005), *The Hitcher* (1986 and 2007), *The Last House on the Left* (1972 and 2009) and *Friday the 13th* (1980 and 2009) which can be just as galling to fans of the originals as the Asian remakes are. It's also interesting to speculate which remakes might actually be worthwhile – *Battle Royale* might play well in the Hebrides, while a Los Angeles/Mexico riff on *Dumplings*, with its satirical skewering of an exploitative culture obsessed with youth and surface appearances, could be a tasty proposition.

INTERACTIVE TERRORS

Given the large stakes Japanese corporations hold in many of the big-name console game manufacturers, it's hardly surprising that the post-*Ring* J-Horrors have exerted a significant influence on the (increasingly cinematic) games – particularly the 'survival-horror' genre, with its complex narratives and emphasis on atmosphere and tension. Interestingly, this style of game began with the Japanese-only release *Sweet Home*, inspired by Kiyoshi Kurosawa's *Poltergeist*-style film of the same name; this game was subsequently revamped as the PS1 game *Resident Evil* – a global smash on its release in 1996 that spawned several American film adaptations, as well as casting a long shadow over the game-playing landscape for the next decade.

In 2001's opening instalment of the multi-platform *Project Zero* survival-horror series (known in the US as *Fatal Frame*), the player takes on the role of a girl exploring an old mansion in search of her missing brother. Pallid *yurei* crop up with alarming regularity, and the game player's only line of defence is an antique *camera obscura* with which they can photograph them, sealing their spirits inside the film. The game's three official sequels are also set in haunted houses or villages, and gradually build up a backstory about Kunihiko Aso, a nineteenth-century occultist who invented a series of devices to gain access to the spirit world. In 2004's PS2 game *Kuon*, set during the medieval Heian period, players guide several sets of characters through a Kyoto mansion infested with mutant monsters to foil the plans of a renegade exorcist. En route, they encounter a spooky set of twins who are revealed as manifestations of evil mulberry trees.

The gold standard for the survival-horror genre was set by the US-set *Silent Hill* franchise, which was drenched in creepy atmospherics and used overlapping planes of reality to build up a complex, evolving plot about a mining town steeped in historical bloodshed and a group of cults called 'The Order' attempting to invoke ancient Lovecraftian deities. The series led to a US film version in 2006, directed by Christophe Gans and starring Radha Mitchell, which owed a significant debt to J-Horror movies. Several of the *Silent Hill* game creators – including director Keiichiro Toyama – went on to mastermind another impressive PS2 game, 2003's *Forbidden Siren* (aka *Siren* in the US), a *Wicker Man*-influenced survival horror set in a remote Japanese mountain village surrounded by blood-red water. The plot shares several elements with the preceding franchise, including its isolated location and the presence of a cult using arcane rituals to summon a supreme deity – in this instance a being known as Datatsushi. The titular 'siren' is this entity's unique call, which impels the village residents to drown themselves in the crimson depths, creating in the process an army of murderous zombies called *shibito* ('corpse people') that the game player must use stealth tactics to avoid. A sequel was created to tie in with the release of the insipid film adaptation, *Forbidden Siren* (2006), which shared its plot. Some of the POV shots from prowling *shibito* were inspired by the game's 'sight-jacking' USP, whereby the game player can commandeer the viewpoint of other characters and creatures for tactical advantage. An English-language adaptation is rumoured to be in production at Sam Raimi and Robert Tapert's Ghost House Pictures.

A memorable *yurei* surfaced – albeit in westernised form – in Vivendi's 2005 first-person shooter *F.E.A.R.* ('First Encounter Assault Recon') where the game player – the point man for a heavily armed US forces special-ops unit tackling paranormal threats – is periodically 'haunted' by the character of Alma Wade. Her blank face obscured by her long black hair, Alma is – in some of her incarnations, at least – a spooky eight-year-old girl (in the mould of *Ring*'s Sadako) who was used as a guinea pig in an experiment to engineer psychic powers. Seeking vengeance on her tormentors, she displays a formidable range of abilities – including liquefying flesh, telekinesis and a habit of dragging characters into an alternative reality where they are stalked by vicious spooks. The player encounters Alma regularly throughout the game, often glimpsing her at the periphery of the frame as she scuttles into the shadows, giggling to herself as a prelude to some gory set-piece. The game's soundtrack also owes a sizable debt to J-Horror films – making effective use of pregnant silences as well as crescendos of atonal industrial noise. The game's official 2009 sequel *F.E.A.R. 2: Project Origin* makes use of similarly atmospheric techniques.

A trilogy of Nintendo games by Konami, based on the *Death Note* films and *mangas*, were released in 2007 and 2008, in which players can adopt the roles of either Kira or 'L' and attempt to flush out their nemesis by investigation and deduction.

Just as video games have influenced the aesthetic of certain films, so a synergy operates whereby film creatives contribute to the games. Ryuhei Kitamura, helmer of the heavily game-influenced *Versus*, directed some of the cinematic cut-scenes and motion-capture sequences for the game *Metal Gear Solid: The Twin Snakes*, while veteran *Battle Royale* director Kinji Fukasaku did the same for Capcom's survival horror *Clock Tower 3*. Shinya Tsukamoto – ever the maverick – performed voice duties for the character Vamp in the 2008 PS3 release *Metal Gear Solid 4*.

REFERENCE WEBSITES

www.midnighteye.com
www.theringworldforum.com
www.loveasianfilm.com
www.horrorview.com
www.asiancult.com
www.hkflix.com
www.evildread.com/asianmacabre
www.kfccinema.com
www.shuqi.org
www.illuminatedlantern.com
www.horrordirectors.com/asia96-02
www.koreanfilm.org

BIBLIOGRAPHY

Balmain, Colette, *Introduction to Japanese Horror Film*, Edinburgh: Edinburgh University Press, 2008

Bush, Laurence C, *Asian Horror Encyclopedia*, Lincoln NE: Writers Club Press, 2001

Carter, David, *East Asian Cinema*, Harpenden: Kamera Books, 2007

Galloway, Patrick, *Asia Shock: Horror and Dark Cinema from Japan, Korea, Hong Kong and Thailand*, Berkeley, CA: Stone Bridge Press, 2006

Harper, Jim, *Flowers From Hell: The Modern Japanese Horror Film*, Hereford: Noir Publishing, 2008

Jones, Alan, *The Rough Guide to Horror Movies*, New York: Rough Guides Ltd, 2005

Kermode, Mark, 'Spirit Levels', *Sight & Sound*, London: BFI, August 2005

McRoy, Jay (ed), *Japanese Horror Cinema*, Edinburgh: Edinburgh University Press, 2005

Mes, Tom & Jasper Sharp (eds), *The Midnight Eye Guide to New Japanese Film*, Berkeley, CA: Stone Bridge Press, 2005

Odell, Colin & Michelle Le Blanc, *Horror Films*, Harpenden: Kamera Books, 2007

Pilkington, Mark & Jule Hartung (eds), *The Tartan Guide to Asia Extreme*, Startlux, 2004

Roddick, Nick, 'Red River', *Sight & Sound*, London: BFI, December 2006

The author is also indebted to the many informative liner notes written for Tartan Asia Extreme releases by Justin Bowyer, Jamie Russell and Calum Waddell.

INDEX

Index

kamera
BOOKS

ESSENTIAL READING FOR ANYONE INTERESTED IN FILM AND POPULAR CULTURE

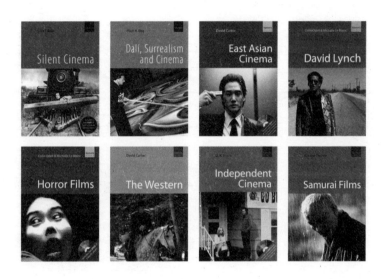

Tackling a wide range of subjects from prominent directors, popular genres and current trends through to cult films, national cinemas and film concepts and theories. Kamera Books include lively, engaged discussion, historical overviews, in-depth film analysis, revealing facts and figures, interviews with filmmakers, comprehensive resources guides to further reading and viewing, and DVDs of shorts, features and documentaries.

www.kamerabooks.com